After the Fall

After the Fall

OPPORTUNITIES AND STRATEGIES FOR REAL ESTATE INVESTING IN THE COMING DECADE

Steve Bergsman

WILEY

John Wiley & Sons, Inc.

Published by John Wiley & Sons, Inc., Hoboken, New Jersey.
Published simultaneously in Canada.

For general information on our other products and services or for technical
support, please contact our Customer Care Department within the United States
at (800) 762-2974, outside the United States at (317) 572-3993 or fax (317)
572-4002.

Wiley also publishes its books in a variety of electronic formats. Some content that
appears in print may not be available in electronic books. For more information
about Wiley products, visit our web site at www.wiley.com.

Library of Congress Cataloging-in-Publication Data:
Bergsman, Steve.
    After the fall : opportunities and strategies for real estate investing in the
coming decade / Steve Bergsman.
        p.   cm.
    Includes bibliographical references and index.
    ISBN 978-0-470-40527-7 (cloth)
    1. Real estate investment.   2. Commercial real estate.   3. Residential real estate.
    I. Title.
    HD1382.5.B466   2009
    332.63'24—dc22

                                                                      2008045558

Printed in the United States of America
10 9 8 7 6 5 4 3 2 1

To my oldest and dearest friend
Ed Moss
who continues to reposition his real estate holdings.

Contents

Acknowledgments

Each book I write is an entirely different process. For my last book project, I found myself shuttling about the world, tracking down sources on Pacific Islands or in thickly forested northlands. In a way I'm embarrassed to admit this, but for *After the Fall: Opportunities and Strategies for Real Estate Investing in the Coming Decade,* I never left my office. Off the top of my head, I can't recall one interview that was face-to-face, and there were many, many interviews done for this book.

This is where longevity pays off. I knew so many players in the real estate and mortgage industries, having written on the subjects for over two decades, that many sources, when asked if they would like to be interviewed over the telephone for this book project, immediately answered yes. For the sources I didn't know, it took a round or two of e-mail correspondence to convince them I was a legitimate writer with a legitimate project. I suppose if they were distrustful, they could have always googled my name to find out my background.

As it turned out, I could count the number of sources on one hand who turned me down. Either they all trusted me or they all had good Internet research skills.

Anyway, a lot of very smart people helped me to write this book, and I wish to acknowledge their help. As always, if I missed mentioning a source, it wasn't on purpose as my intention is to thank each and every one for sharing knowledge, experience, and market insights.

In order of appearance: Mitchell Hersh, Sam Chandon, Dan Fasulo, David Twardock, Douglas Shorenstein, Robert Bach, Colleen McPherson, Mark Weinberg, Luciana Suran, Michael McKiernan, Brad Copeland, Leonard Sahling, Michael Dermody, Charles Schreiber, Kevin Wilkerson, Matthew Anderson, Jim Koury, Sam Davis, Chauncey Mayfield, Dan Ansell, Christopher Volk, Richard Moore, Michael Pollack, Peter Donovan, Matthew Lawton, Richard

Campo, Greg Willet, Gleb Nechayev, Lisa Sarajian, George Skoufis, Richard McBlaine, Jay Biggins, Dan Rashin, Jason Hartke, Mark Palmer, Anthony Irons, Matt Garlinghouse, Nicholas Eisenberger, Christopher Desloge, Olivia Millar, Nicholas Stolatis, Lauralee Martin, J. Allen Smith, Carlos Martin, Douglas Wilson, Matt Wanderer, David Tobin, Gil Tenzer, Russell Bernard, Ray Milnes, Richard Berry, Spencer Garfield, Pat Ford, Jack Corgel, Mark Woodworth, Kapila Anand, Ted Mandigo, Glenn Schultz, Peter Hooper, Jared Sullivan, Jonathan Dienhart, Richard DeKaser, Jed Smith, Celia Chen, Mel Gamzon, Robert Kramer, Raymond Lewis, David Schless, Richard Swerdlow, Walter Molony, Jack McCabe, Brian Gordon, Mario Greco, Brad Capas, Jules Marling, Robert Hartwig, Terry Butler, J. Robert Hunter, Eric Goldberg, Alex Winter, Paula Aschettino, Dennis Burke, Charlie Melancon, Natalia Siniavskaia, Elliott Eisenberg, Gerald Prante, Bert Waisanen, Charles Longino, Don Bradley, Gary Engelhardt, David Goldberg, Douglas Bibby, Charles Leinberger, Arthur C. Nelson, John McIlwain, Tom Booher, Bob Moss, Andrew Weil, Michael Novogradac, Nicolas Retsinas, Howard Nussbaum, Ed Kinney, Christine Karpinski, Liam Bailey, Ron Baron, William Van Gelder, Pat Kelly, Mark Lunt, Robert Goldstein, Jared Beck, Jamie Cheng, Nick Copley, Michel Neutelings, and Alfredo Merat.

Introduction

Around mid-year 2006, I was chatting with an acquaintance at a local coffee shop and he was telling me the story of a friend of his in California who had strung together a series of home purchases. She would buy one home, take a second mortgage on the property, then use the money from the second to acquire another property. She was so successful at this game that she had accumulated something like a dozen Southern California properties; all but one (where she lived) were rentals. It didn't appear the rental rates were covering the mortgages, but that was all right to the woman because home values were skipping higher every month. On paper she looked like a millionaire.

My friend, who was a successful businessman, wasn't entirely comfortable with his friend's real estate position and asked me what she should do. I told him the outlook for residential real estate had turned sour and she should start selling as quickly as possible.

In retrospect, if she had followed my advice, she probably would have escaped the collapse of the residential real estate market in 2007. But, to illustrate how brilliant I really am as a pundit, that same year, I found myself being interviewed by a local publication and was asked what I thought about the subprime mortgage market, which was suddenly making a lot of people nervous. My response went something like this: Subprime only represents a small portion of the mortgage market. Factually, I was right, but my implied message was off the mark.

Such is the soothsaying business these days. If you get right 50 percent of whatever you might be divining these days, you should consider yourself lucky.

This is what no one predicted: When the residential real estate market bubble finally burst as it did in 2007, the collapse would be so sudden, so quick, and so deep, that a little over a year later it would mean the end of the independent investment bank, an institution that dominated Wall Street since the Glass-Steagall Act of 1933.

Here's a journalist's story on how fast the collapse came. In June 2007, I was asked by my editor at *Mortgage Banking* magazine to write a story on Tucson, Arizona-based First Magnus Financial Corp., which was one of the country's largest privately held mortgage companies. Earlier that year, *National Mortgage News* ranked First Magnus as the ninth largest Alt-A lender in the country with $2.6 billion in volume.

The story was written, edited, and ready to be published when in August First Magnus filed for bankruptcy protection. In less than two months, it went from a successful entrepreneurial company with over 5,000 employees and a bright tomorrow to nothing. The company evaporated over the course of six weeks, and First Magnus executives never saw it coming. When I spoke with them in June, the future was written in hi-liter colors all over their faces.

In the course of interviewing people for this book, when picking out the culprits of the great real estate mortgage industry devaluation, a number of sources mentioned the press. I thought that was a bit unfair, not only because I'm a journalist, but for a couple of years starting around 2005 and certainly through 2006, many financial publications were calling the crazy, rampant housing sector a bubble that was about to burst.

"Bubble, bubble!" the columnists called out, quoting market analysts, investors, hedge fund execs, and equity market decision makers. And, of course, it's all toil and trouble now—so much for bubble, bubble.

As a scribe who writes for almost a dozen different real estate and financial publications on a regular basis, I've personally written dozens of stories about the impending bursting of the housing bubble. Now I wonder who read those articles.

Not being an industry insider, I wonder what happens when you sense the end of the good times is nigh. Judging from what happened to lenders, homebuilders, Wall Street, big banks, and so on, I guess you do nothing and keep running forward for as fast and as far as you can before everything collapses around you.

At some point, do you say to yourself, it looks like the end of the run and we should begin to scale back. Or, is the forward momentum so great that it is just too hard to put on the brakes, let alone reverse direction?

When Ralph Cioffi and Matthew Tannin, two former Bear Stearns hedge fund managers, were arrested in 2008 and indicted on conspiracy and securities fraud charges, in my heart I wanted to say it was unfair that two people should be singled out for the company's folly, but truth be told I had no sympathy for them. Cioffi said (on record!), "I knew the party was over, especially for residential mortgages," but neither he nor Tannin could bring themselves to stop selling mortgage-backed securities investments. After years of pitching this stuff to investors worldwide, they just couldn't stop—the forward momentum was too great.

The other thing that no one predicted was that the subprime mortgage collapse would not be a limited sector event. Much to everyone's shock, subprime ended up to be a virulent, financial contagion infecting banking systems, investment markets, and all real estate sectors worldwide. It was the flu epidemic of the financial world. Over a period of a few short days in September 2008, three major financial firms went down. Lehman Brothers filed for bankruptcy, Merrill Lynch was acquired, and insurer AIG needed to be bailed out by the federal government.

Considering all the inaccurate punditry, what made me want to try my hand at predicting what would happen to the various real estate sectors after the onset of the residential mortgage crisis, shaken financial sector, ensuing credit crisis, slowing economy, property value depreciation, and any other sad issues one might want to throw into the mixer?

The answer is *when* bubbles burst and market sectors fall apart, the knee-jerk reaction is always to say something to the effect, "Okay, we've got a problem, but it will be short-lived." I'm not sure why people who should know better say that, when all evidence suggests otherwise. I could understand the reassurance factor, but where is the credibility? When bubbles burst, the effects almost always last a long time. When real estate bubbles deflate, it is never a short-term problem.

Although I hesitate to admit this, when the last great real estate recession struck at the end of the 1980s, I was doing what I'm still doing, writing about property and financial markets. Although that recession was different in that it was led by commercial real estate overbuilding instead of residential real estate overlending, essentially when it comes down to it, we are talking about the same thing: too much liquidity in the system, which overstimulates investment and drives values up falsely.

A time-line summation of that property crash and recovery shows about three years in the trough and then another three years to clean up the markets and reset values. By year seven, financial systems and real estate markets get back to normal.

Although that is a very general model, my guess was that the time consequences would repeat again in this current real estate downturn. Despite all those assurances, my gut reaction was that this downtrodden real estate market—and I'm including the mortgage end of the system as well—would take a long time to get back to normal.

Knowing that all real estate sectors act differently and all geographic markets move on different time lines, I nevertheless decided to undertake this book project—what to expect from real estate over the next few years and into the coming decade—because sudden, wrenching, often very negative change in markets creates opportunities. Smart investors read the future in the carnage.

To write the book, I turned to everyone I knew in the industry and many people I knew of but had never spoken with in the past.

The tone and accent of this book, as revealed by each chapter title, would focus on an individual asset class such as office, industrial, multifamily, and so on. But as I was writing, other issues and other asset types turned up so I added them as bonuses (actually bonus boxes) in each chapter. Some issues were obviously a kind of "megatrend" (e.g., the Green revolution and infill development), so I carved out new chapters for those subjects as well.

What I sidestepped was government legislation as there were a tremendous number of federal initiatives being bandied about over the course of writing this book, but none had become law. Since I couldn't guess which bill would pass and in what format, I stuck strictly to market forces.

Of course, what readers want to know is "When will real estate markets come back?" Since I'm not a soothsayer, I don't know that answer, but what I tried to do is script a time line for individual real estate sectors based on historical paths, movement of data fundamentals, market analysis, and collective opinion. After wading through all that, I do indicate for many sectors when I believe the trough will finally be reached, how long the climb back will take, when the next peak will occur, and, unfortunately, play taps for those asset classes that physically, mentally, and economically will be scraped away.

Much to my surprise, *After the Fall: Opportunities and Strategies for Real Estate Investing in the Coming Decade* ended up being much more comprehensive than I had intended. I took that to be a good thing. But who could have predicted it?

After the Fall

PART
I

COMMERCIAL REAL ESTATE

CHAPTER ONE

THE OFFICE MARKET

Steady fundamentals; This sector will bifurcate into have and have-not metros

"The office market is going nowhere—fast," observes Mitchell Hersh, president and chief executive officer of Mack-Cali Realty Corporation.

Hersh should know a thing or two about the office market as his company, based in Edison, New Jersey, ranks as one of the largest real estate investment trusts, or REITs, that owns, develops, and manages office buildings. In the first quarter of 2008, Mack-Cali revenues totaled just over $800 million.

I have never met Mitchell Hersh, but he and I have spoken many times over the past years. I would have thought he would be more optimistic about the markets considering the fact that in 2007 he shrewdly increased Mack-Cali's liquidity by issuing over a quarter of a billion dollars in new equity in a secondary offering and then in the third quarter increased the company's credit facility by $175 million—all before the commercial real estate market, following the residential markets, froze up. Mack-Cali's portfolio of properties (almost all of which were located in the Northeast) going into 2008 was about 93 percent occupied.

As he liked to say, "His powder was dry," in case potential deals arose. And he expected to see substantial opportunities to acquire in the years ahead as badly financed office buildings will definitely need to be dumped back onto the market.

Over the previous decade, a vast amount of institutional capital had been created from the aging baby boomers, who had money in pension funds and 401(k)s. All this money had to be invested somewhere. After the dot-com bust of the late 1990s, much of this money found its way to commercial real estate, including office buildings.

So much competition for good prices forced down yields. "I cannot give you the exact snapshot," Hersh says, "but yields went from 6 percent to just over 3 percent in about 18 months. Yes, the cost of capital was cheap and interest rates fairly low, but the investments were all about expectations."

The theory was that U.S. cities such as New York, Boston, and Washington, D.C., were global communities and rents, as compared to overseas capital centers such as London and Tokyo, were inexpensive by comparison. Ultimately, a repricing had to occur. With a limited amount of new supply coming online, if the investor was acquiring property at a 2.5 or 3 percent yield, it was all right because if rents were $100 a square foot today, they should be $200 a square foot tomorrow, and that would grow the investor out of his low-yield problem.

Actually what happened, says Hersh, was that investors, even if they had capital, because cheap money was available, leveraged their investments. Not only did they secure traditional first-mortgage financing, but added to the debt stack with short-term mezzanine debt and bridge loans. Then they waited for these explosive rents to grow and bail them out. "The notion was in New York, if you bought at $1,200 a square foot, two or three years later you could sell at $2,000 a square and in effect you could flip out of the property," he explained to me.

Unfortunately, rents have stalled and will continue to retract. "2007 was the best performing year and the peak of the office market in terms of fundamentals," notes Sam Chandon, chief economist and senior vice president of REIS Inc., the New York real estate research firm. But most of that performance occurred by the second quarter, when asking rents for office markets nationally jumped

9.6 percent, and on an effective basis, 10.7 percent. In the third quarter of 2007 came the residential real estate subprime blowout, followed by the onset of the credit crunch and a series of crises for U.S. financial firms and all those gains began heading in the opposite direction.

"There is no doubt office building prices escalated to the point where many investors had to justify significant rent increases in the first few years of ownership to make pro formas work," notes Dan Fasulo, managing director of research at Real Capital Analytics, the New York–based research company.

"Investors really started to expect high rent increases in 2005 and 2006, and for the most part the early investors got the rents they were seeking. It was only the investors at the tail end of 2006 through the middle of 2007 who will have a difficult time getting the rents they need.

"Certainly rental rates are not increasing anymore at the pace they were several years ago," Fasulo adds, "Actually, as of the first quarter 2008 in many markets across the United States, there is evidence rates have dropped and concessions are increasing."

Hersh adds with dismay, "A lot of expectations won't be met and the day of reckoning is going to be in front of us."

In February 2008, the *Wall Street Journal* spotlighted the very large New York suburban office market of North-Central New Jersey, in the heart of the Mack-Cali's investment footprint. Statistically, there were two items of note: From fourth quarter 2006 to fourth quarter 2007, average annual rent per square foot moved from $24.62 to $25.54, a carryover from the buoyant office market before the subprime blowout; and over the same period of time, the office vacancy rate held steady at 17.8 percent, a not very strong number.[1]

The *Journal* noted, "Even as the area's average office rents are ticking up, the region is facing the headwinds of a potential national recession."[2] The newspaper then cited layoffs in the pharmaceutical sector (a big employer in the area) and stagnant job growth.

The harbinger of a troubled market came from the observation that sales of large commercial buildings in the region had come to a grinding halt. Referencing Real Capital Analytics data, the *Journal* reported overall sales of office, retail, warehouse, and apartment properties valued at $5 million or more dropped more than 75 percent, from the same quarter a year earlier to $811 million. Northern

New Jersey had tied Sacramento and Kansas City, Missouri, for the largest percentage drop of 50 major U.S. markets.

Where We Are Today

After the dot-com bust at the beginning of the new millennium, a lot of capital that had gone into the stock market, in particular high technology companies, began to migrate to other investments, such as commercial real estate, that appeared to be more stable. Beginning in 2002 and 2003, a huge wave of capital flooded into investments like office properties and shopping centers where individual units were under long-term leases to credit tenants. In that period of time, the volume of acquisitions rose to a stunning $50 billion annually.

Investors soon realized that for many commercial real estate asset classes, such as office buildings, there were further attractions. There had been limited new construction since the last real estate recession in the early 1990s, the sector wasn't overbuilt, and a smart investment could capture improving fundamentals. Dealmaking really began to take off. Real Capital Analytics reported $140 billion in office building sales in 2006, followed by a record $215 billion in office building sales in 2007.

However, 2007 ended up to be a bifurcated year as most of the record transactions occurred before the subprime blowup in the summer of that year.

The frantic pace of dealmaking just in the office sector was so pronounced that even conservative institutional investors, such as pension funds, threw out their guidebooks and dived into the maelstrom. Institutional investors, including REITs, pension plans, insurance companies, and even opportunity funds, are known as long-term holders of real estate, sitting on their investments for at least 7 to 10 years. But their holding periods dropped to five to seven years and in many cases two to five years.

There was so much capital flowing into the office sector, the price per square foot skyrocketed to record levels, then new record levels. In fact, a number of itchy-finger investors realized buildings could be bought for millions of dollars one day, then a few months later flipped for even greater millions.

In 2006, I began writing a story for *Barron's* magazine, with these comments: "It's not just your old college roommate, the one who never held a steady job, who is buying and selling real estate faster than he can down a *mojito* at a Miami Beach bar. Institutional investors have caught the heat as well. Big office buildings and apartment communities are changing hands sometimes before the sign that says 'new owner' has been nailed to the wall. Everyone seems to be focused on the crazed condominiums markets in places like Las Vegas and Miami Beach, but institutional real estate investments are often trading equally as fast."[3]

At the time, I mentioned how a group of New York investors bought the San Francisco trophy property Bank of America Center in 2004 for $825 million, and when I was writing the story in the autumn of 2006, it was back on the market with an asking price of $1.25 billion.

My favorite example of office building flipping was the 185,000-square-foot office building at 485 Fifth Avenue in New York. It sold in 1995 at $137 a square foot, sold in 2000 at $180 (or $200 depending on your source) a square foot, sold in 2004 at approximately $295 a square foot, and sold in 2005 at approximately $475 a square foot.[4]

Perhaps the greatest flip was the Blackstone Group acquisition of Equity Office Properties Trust, the largest office REIT in the country, for $39 million. Over half of the portfolio was immediately flipped to other investors. The Blackstone deal marked the peak of the office acquisition frenzy.

Sam Zell, former founder and chairman of Equity Office Properties Trust, is known as one of the savviest real estate investors in the world, having among other successes founded three REITs: Equity Office Properties Trust, Equity Residential Properties Trust, and Manufactured Home Communities Inc. However, Equity Office Properties Trust ended up on the auction block because of a rare boneheaded investment by Zell. In 2001, Equity Office closed on the $7.3 billion acquisition of another office REIT—Spieker Properties Inc.

The idea behind the deal was rational. Spieker was a major investor in Northern California and especially San Francisco, where Equity Office was weak. Unfortunately, the deal was completed just as the dot.com bubble deflated, throwing a lot of empty office space back into the market. Equity Office never regained its momentum and over the next years the company lost investor favor. It was obvious to aggressive equity players such as Blackstone that the market was undervaluing the high quality of Equity Office's huge portfolio of buildings.

In my first book, *Maverick Real Estate Investing: The Art of Buying and Selling Properties like Trump, Zell, Simon and the World's Greatest Land Owners,* I began by writing that great investors exhibit unbelievable patience. They never rush into deals and wait out market cycles even if it takes years. Six long years after the Spieker blunder, Zell finally struck back, engineering an intense bidding competition between Blackstone and Vornado Realty Trust for his company, just when the market for office buildings was in a culminating, frothing frenzy.

At no time in the years before and certainly at no time in the near future would Zell have been able to sell Equity Office at such a propitious moment. The timing was perfect, because just a few months later, the residential subprime market exploded.

The Blackstone folks were no fools. They immediately flipped billions of dollars worth of the office buildings, thus paying down a great deal of the debt taken on by the transaction.

When flipping starts, the investment market begins to take on all the characteristics of musical chairs, except in the children's game when the music stops, the last child sitting is the winner. In the flipping game, when markets collapse, the last investor sitting or standing is the loser.

The most famous investor to get caught as the last investor on the Blackstone flip was New York real estate magnate Harry Macklowe, who as I'm writing this chapter, was struggling to find a way to save his empire. His problem was he bought $7 billion of the Equity Office assets from Blackstone, which he paid for with short-term debt, thinking he would be able to quickly refinance those loans with long-term financing. The credit markets fell apart in the wake of the subprime meltdown before he could do so, and those short-term loans came due. To drum up cash, Macklowe put up for sale the jewel in his holdings, the GM Building in Manhattan.

Another investor who was still standing when the music stopped was the Kushner Companies of Florham Park, New Jersey, which paid $1.8 billion for a 41-story office tower at 666 Fifth Avenue in Manhattan in 2007. Not only was this more than three times what the building sold for in 2000, but at the time it was the highest price paid for a single building in the United States. For the acquisition, the Kushner Companies was able to get an interest-only mortgage of $1.215 billion, and then like Macklowe relied on short-term debt to bridge the difference between that number and equity.[5]

And like Macklowe, when the bridge loan came due, the credit markets were already in turmoil, and it couldn't be financed. But Kushner had sold a large portfolio of apartment units and was able to pay off a $200 million loan.[6] The important thing to note in this deal, besides the grand price tag of the building, was that cash flow from existing rents would actually cover only 65 percent of the debt service. That amounted to a shortfall of $5 million a month.[7] Like other investors, the Kushner Companies was relying on a buoyant real estate market to make up the difference. That was in 2007, but even two years earlier when I was writing my "flipping" article for *Barron's,* Lloyd Lynford, CEO of REIS, told me that buyers had already become "overly aggressive," according to a REIS company report that compared cash flow potential (actual value) of an investment against transaction price. The result was what REIS calls the "premium" being paid; for office buildings, that premium bulged to about 33 percent (over actual value).[8]

That brings us back to Macklowe, who as of spring 2008, was trying to sell the GM Building for over $3.5 billion. This fact led the *Wall Street Journal* to rhapsodize that the GM Building "so bewitches investors that it's difficult to determine if the high bids say more about the strength of the New York office market or about the motives of the people who covet it. After all, the rents from the building barely pay the mortgage and many tenants have long-term leases far below current rates. Yet, the sales price jumps every time it changes hands."[9]

As one observer noted, "Nobody ever made money owning the General Motors Building; they only made money selling it."[10]

Maybe Boston Properties Inc. will. In June 2008, it bought the GM Building for $2.8 billion, including assumption of debt.[11]

Where We Were

Over the past two decades, the United States has experienced a couple of short recessions following key incidents such as the collapse of the $4 billion hedge fund Long Term Capital Management, which kicked off a global financial crisis, and then again after the terrorist attacks in 2001. The deepest real estate recession of recent times began in the late 1980s and continued to roil property markets well into the early 1990s. In some regards the genesis of that real estate recession was similar to that of one that began in 2007: too much capital floating around the market.

Basically, coming out of the 1970s, tremendous tax incentives were in place for building commercial real estate and huge amounts of new product started hitting the market. Then the Tax Reform Act of 1986 took away many of the deductions for this irresponsible building. Compounding the problem was a modification of the regulations governing savings and loans, allowing them to compete better with commercial banks, and the thrifts jumped madly into commercial real estate lending. The eventual outcome of all this was tremendously overbuilt property markets, the collapse of the savings and loan industry, the creation of the federal government's Resolution Trust Corporation to help solve the problem, and the establishment of the commercial mortgage-backed securities industry.

To get an idea of how much building went on, a look at just the office sector shows that from 1981 to 1989 over 100 million square feet of new space was created annually, with almost 200 million square feet in 1985 alone, reports REIS Inc. By the time the commercial real estate market hit bottom, less than 10 million square feet had been built in 1993 and 1994. The office market slowly began to reconstruct until the dot-com boom hit at the end of the 1990s, according to REIS data, and new office construction rose to over 100 million square feet again for the three years from 1999 to 2001.

From 2003 to 2007, two trend lines emerged. New construction moderated, REIS reports, ranging from 28 million square feet to 70 million square feet over those years, and cheap capital ignited an acquisition frenzy. In 2002 and 2003 fundamentals began to come back to the sector and that, combined with a real lack of oversupply, sparked investor interest. In the office sector, transaction volume moved above the $50 billion market for the first time, jumping all the way to $74 billion in 2004, notes Real Capital Analytics. The numbers then climbed exponentially to $105 billion in 2005, $138 billion in 2006, and $215 billion in 2007.

If too much liquidity helped create the real estate recession in the late 1980s, the same holds true for 2007, but with great differences. The liquidity in the 1980s flowed into development schemes, whereas in the years after the turn of the century it was used for dealmaking.

Where We Are Headed

The record amount of office deals in 2007 was partially fueled by Blackstone's acquisition of Equity Office and subsequent flipping of properties. According to Real Capital Analytics, these deals alone accounted for $66 billion of sales that year. If there was anything unusual in all of this, it was that those particular markets heavy with Equity Office properties saw some of those individual properties trade two or three times over the course of 2007, thus making those markets some of the most active.

In 2007, 35 markets recorded more than $1 billion worth of office property sales. Manhattan remained the most active market nationwide with over $40 billion in sales, four times the volume of the next highest market. Los Angeles retained the top spot for the most individual properties sold, with 236 in 2007.

According to Real Capital Analytics, the top 10 locations with the heaviest sales volume, in descending order were Manhattan, $40.9 billion; San Francisco, $12.4 billion; Los Angeles, $12 billion; Chicago, $11.7 billion; Seattle, $11.2 billion; DC-Virginia suburbs, $10.7 billion; Boston, $9.1 billion; Orange County (California), $6.9 billion; Houston, $6.3 billion; and the District of Columbia, $6 billion.

Although the Equity Office acquisition skewed the geography of office deals, it was, however, an indicator of what is ahead in the office sector. Over the next few years, the United States will become a have and have-not marketplace for office investors. Those cities with less perceived risk will attract capital and those with the perception of risk (called second- and third-tier cities) will not.

What makes one city more "risky" than another is fewer barriers to entry. One reason why places like Manhattan, San Francisco, and the District of Columbia remain popular for office investors is that it is so very difficult to find vacant land to build a new project. In these dense cities, an old property will have to come down before anything new can be constructed, thus making new building even more expensive. If there are extreme barriers to entry, only a moderate amount of new offices are introduced into the market, making competition intense and keeping rents high. At least that's the theory.

Before I began this book, I interviewed David Twardock, president of Prudential Mortgage Capital Company, a Prudential Financial Inc. unit, for a story I was writing for *Mortgage Banking* magazine. With the commercial mortgage-backed securities (CMBS) market eviscerated, about the only lenders left in the game during 2008 were the insurance companies, which were portfolio lenders. They kept their investments in portfolios rather than securitizing them and selling pieces to other investors.

Early in 2008, Twardock wasn't a big fan of the office market, but he was willing to invest on a strict geographic basis. "There are few office markets that have been really good," he said. "If you get down to it, New York, Boston, and if you bought at the right time, maybe San Francisco and Los Angeles. A lot of the other markets were never there—never very much in terms of cash flow increases. That is why some of the office REITs (like Equity Office) that are in select markets do well. With the financial service companies facing some issues, some of these markets will be weak for the next two to three years."

In the midst of 2007, the wildest year in the history of the U.S. office market, where a record volume of properties changed hands, there were already geographic divergences occurring. Almost every major city showed an increase in sales volume from 2006 to 2007, except Dallas (–34%), Boston (–25%), Atlanta (–12%), and San Jose (–6%), reports Real Capital Analytics. With all that activity, as one could imagine, the average price per square foot was leaping madly upward, but here too, there were laggards. From 2006 to 2007, the price per square foot dropped in Boston (–26%), San Fancisco (–23%), Chicago (–8%), Atlanta (–2%), and Los Angeles, Dallas, Phoenix, and Houston (all –1%).

In terms of yield, as defined by average capitalization rate (present value of a stream of future earnings arrived at by dividing normalized earnings after taxes by present value), most markets saw a huge decline. With so much competition to buy properties, lower cap rates are expected. Again, there were slips here as well; between 2006 and 2007, Boston and Phoenix experienced a rise in cap rates.

"There was, on a relative basis, a surge in transactions over the last couple of years (through 2007), now in 2008 there is nothing happening because of the cap rate corrections, which are more pricing corrections, in those cities where there is no liquidity," says REIS's Chandon. "People are willing to pay for liquidity and show up to buy properties in New York and Los Angeles, but not in places like Chattanooga. In second- and third-tier cities there is no liquidity and there is no exit strategy for office building investors."

"There will be a bifurcation between markets considered global and markets dependent on the U.S. domestic economy," adds Real Capital's Fasulo. "Second-tier cities, many in the Midwest, are going to act much differently than Manhattan, which has a global diversification element. Growth in Manhattan will come from international business. Meanwhile, here in the United States, business is plateauing. Cities with a global business environment like New York; Washington, D.C.; San Francisco are not facing the same problems as, for example, a St. Louis."

The impact of the credit crisis brought on by the subprime blowout was so quick that by the end of 2007 the main driver of office market acquisition activity, conduit loans (pooled, diced by ratings, and then sold as commercial mortgage-backed securities) had completely collapsed. The drying up of liquidity depressed the office market immediately and between the summer of 2007 and the advent of spring 2008, average prices fell nationally around 10 to 15 percent. The expectations are that prices will slow as the liquidity shock gets absorbed. Conservative estimates for office building pricing (on an average national basis) are that they will drop no more than another 5 percent.

"If the country enters a minor recession," says Fasulo, "I would be very surprised if office market pricing lost another 10 percent. It would take a global recession to push this down even further." Fasulo's worst case scenario came to pass as bourses collapsed and credit markets froze up in almost all countries across the globe by the third quarter 2008.

Fundamentals

In terms of operations, there is good news and bad news ahead for office properties. Unlike the great real estate recession of the early 1990s, this time around one of the main factors causing markets to implode is not overbuilding. The last burst of building activity, where national completions topped 100 million square feet was during the dot-com bubble. Since then, according to REIS, new construction mirrored, if not drifted below, demand, and national vacancy rates slowly declined from 17 percent in 2003 to 12.2 percent in 2007.

One result of that was steadily rising rents.

Chandon believes that this trend line will continue well into the next decade. According to REIS, new construction will stay moderate, maybe topping 50 million square feet in any given year, whereas net absorption, which took a big hit in 2008, will return again and then continue to rise through 2012. In Chandon's view, vacancy rates will start to decline again after 2009 and rental rates should get back on a winning track.

That's the economists' point of view, but the outlook from people in the trenches is not so rosy. Although not disagreeing with the economists, the folks who own and manage office properties expect to see considerable pain inflicted on those investors who thought office properties were as good as gold.

Unfortunately, the price of gold fluctuates and so do the fortunes of office properties.

"In 2007, the frenzy in the office market was so great, it was like day-trading," observes Douglas Shorenstein, chairman and CEO of Shorenstein Properties LLC, a San Francisco private real estate investment company active in the development and management of office and mixed-use properties. "The values were not tied to historic real estate fundamentals like cash flow. It was more a factor of who would bid the highest price. You had auctions where 25 credible bidders showed and the bidding blew right through economic fundamentals. People were just trying to place capital."

"The basic business of the office property is leasing," says Shorenstein, explaining Office Management 101, a course most investors seem to have slept through. "This is the revenue side of the business and underpins the real estate."

When I spoke with Shorenstein in spring 2008, he was seeing the leasing market begin to soften. Obviously, the biggest enemy of commercial properties is vacancies, because losing a tenant means loss of cash flow. In a down market, it gets very expensive to keep occupancy up because other buildings offer cheaper deals so tenants crank up the requests for improvements. It gets very expensive to maintain occupancy in a soft market.

Although investors were buying office buildings at crazy prices up until 2007, increased rental rates were bailing the investors out. Shorenstein laughs, "At one point in the cycle, vacant buildings were worth more than buildings with leases in place under the theory that any new lease would be higher than any lease that was in place. I had never seen anything like this in my career."

In 2008, the only lenders left in the market were balance sheet lenders and to them it was all about fundamentals, not expected appreciation.

Capital was, indeed, cheap until 2007, and lots of deals were done with inexpensive securitized debt. However, taking advantage of the liquid capital markets, investors capped off the securitized debt that was 70 to 80 percent loan-to-value with mezzanine or bridge loans, which is expensive short-term debt. If that debt is coming due, investors have a problem. There is no access to new equity and those loans will go into default. There will be blood.

Bonus Box

The Office Condominium

For a long time, whenever I gave a talk about real estate investments to novice and local investors, I would often recommend the development of a small office building with enough space for two to four tenants. Frankly, I was a little behind the times because the office condominium (buy the space, not lease it) began to take up that niche. I really should have known better because I live in Mesa, Arizona, just outside Phoenix, and this central Arizona metro area had become the epicenter of the office condo world, with more of the product in place and under development than anywhere else in the country.

When I first wrote about the office condo phenomenon early in 2006, Phoenix already had more than 6.5 million square feet of office space built and 4.9 million square feet planned. This was at a time when many cities hadn't experienced a first office condo. Dallas, for example, which boasts a much bigger office market than Phoenix, could count just two office condo projects completed at the time.

This certainly looked like the coming trend, but when I had to write a second national office condominium market story for *National Real Estate Investor* magazine at the end of that same year, I called Robert Bach, who headed research for the Grubb & Ellis Co. and had recently done a report on the niche market. He was not very positive. In fact, his comment to me at the time (the close of 2006) was that the burgeoning office condo trend was merely a temporary phenomenon powered by low interest rates.

At the time, I wasn't sure he was right, but two years later his words proved prophetic.

When I first wrote about the office condo market in Phoenix, I passed over a firm called Shea Commercial because it wasn't quick enough to get back to me. After the story came out, Jim Riggs,

Continued

(*Continued*)

president of the company, called me up and cussed me out for leaving him out of the story as his company was "the largest office condo developer in the country." So, when I began writing about office condos for this chapter, the first person I called was Jim Riggs. He never returned my telephone calls.

The second person I called was Colleen McPherson, vice president of office for CB Richard Ellis Inc.'s Phoenix office and a person who tracked the office condo market. When I told her about Riggs not returning my phone calls, she replied that was because this niche product was in foul shape and all the local office condo developers "were in trouble."

I didn't get to talk long with McPherson, but I had seen comments she made in other publications. According to McPherson, the original wave of office condos in the Phoenix area that sold in the late 1990s to early 2000s hit the market at about $170 a square foot. Eventually, prices climbed to $250 and $300 a square foot. By 2008, after the credit crunch, the prices dropped back to $200 a square foot. One big problem, she noted, was that buyers of office condos do not want built-out space.[12]

Other markets such as Miami-Dade County were experiencing similar trends.[13] On the other hand, a close friend acquired an office condo in Orange County, California, near John Wayne Airport, and when asked, he told me the development was steadily filling up. Orange County's office market at the time sported a gaudy 30 percent vacancy rate, which meant there was a lot of inexpensive space on the market—tough competition for office condo developers.

I still maintain that office condos are a useful product for a small service company needing 5,000 square feet or less, but it is a relatively new phenomenon; and therefore the secondary market has not established any track record. Buy an office condo if it fits your company needs, but as a pure investment it will take another decade to sort out this niche.

CHAPTER TWO

THE INDUSTRIAL MARKET

It's all about massive distribution facilities; Corporate America is not distributing its largesse evenly across the country

After the dot-com blowup at the turn of the millennium, the industrial real estate market went askew. For four consecutive years, 2001 through 2004, the average vacancy rate on the national level ran at double digits. Depending on whose numbers you look at, the very worst year was 2003, when vacancies climbed all the way to 11 percent.

Eleven percent! In the office sector, when a city gets down to 11 percent it's considered a healthy market. Already some communities are exhibiting office vacancies in the 20 to 25 percent range. When we look at something like 11 percent in industrial, we wonder where's the panic? This is especially so when in the best years, vacancy rates are generally in the 7+ percent range.

The difference between bad years and good years in industrial real estate is often less than 4 percent. Industrial is the savings bond of real estate investing: safe, stable, and relatively boring.

"It is one of the more stable assets in commercial real estate as it does not fluctuate up or down as much as office or retail. It's more akin to the apartment business in terms of risk profile," notes Brad Copeland, a director at ING Clarion, a firm that has been very active in acquiring industrial real estate assets.

Two things to like about industrial real estate: It has stable cash flow, and it is kind of a defensive investment when real estate markets are in turmoil.

So, it's very surprising that when we look at trend lines unwinding into the future, there is no real estate asset class more cutting edge or undergoing more change than industrial space. The reason for this has less to do with basic real estate investing and more to do with the changing operations of Corporate America.

Where We Are

For most companies, supply chains (from manufacturer to a shelf at a store near you) are longer and more convoluted. As I noted—with some exaggeration—in a 2008 article for *Chief Executive* magazine: For any given product, raw materials can be sourced in Africa, refined in India, partly manufactured in China, assembled in Mexico and finally distributed in the United States.[1]

Not only are supply chains confusing but they are expensive to maintain. The costly manufacturing piece of the chain can be attacked by getting work done in low-wage countries such as China, but it has become harder to control the transportation part of the process. When the price of oil blows past $100 a barrel, that means the cost of production has certainly risen, but it also means a huge increase in the expense to transport parts, materials, and completed goods.

Some of these costs are passed along to consumers, but in many cases the market is too competitive to raise prices so companies have to look at the total supply chain, not just manufacturing but logistics as well.

This is where industrial buildings come into play: Industrial real estate no longer exists as a separate asset class, but is part of the whole reengineering of a corporate business.

"Transportation, labor, and real estate are the three main costs of distribution," notes Mark Weinberg, a senior managing director with Newmark Knight Frank, "so real estate decisions are increasingly being viewed as strategic decisions within organizations."

Since we now manufacture more goods overseas than ever before, here in the United States companies have to figure out how to quickly and effectively get product (including raw materials for goods manufactured here) from foreign shores into the country and finally to a store near you.

Import volume, reports Luciana Suran, an economist with CBRE/Torto Wheaton Research, is more highly correlated with distribution/warehouse net absorption than export volume and imports, which by almost any measure are twice to two-thirds higher than exports.

Organizationally, many firms have gone to just-in-time business strategies that reduce inventory and associated carrying costs. To do that, companies need an efficient flow of goods and that usually falls under the rubric of distribution.

In terms of real estate, the lexicon follows exactly and this is where Corporate America is focusing its efforts on distribution facilities. The official category often gets referred to as warehouse/distribution, but due to the actual nature of business in these facilities, many are separating the category into two asset classes: warehouse *and* distribution. "There is now a difference in the concept of warehouse and the concept of distribution," avers Michael McKiernan, executive managing director of industrial brokerage with Cushman & Wakefield. "Warehouse connotes more slowly moving inventory. A distribution center is designed for the temporary housing of a product and its quick dissemination."

While Newmark Knight Frank calls itself a full-service real estate company, Weinberg's job goes beyond just the property brokerage sphere. Not only is it his job to help companies find the optimal place for a distribution center but also to aid in design: size of buildings, shape, number of docks, interior flow-through, clearheight, space utilization, and peak storage capacity. Distribution centers look simple, but placement and design get complicated.

Weinberg focuses so intensely on all aspects of the structure because distribution facilities are the present and the future for industrial property markets. This is the product Corporate America is building at the moment. It's the property that investors want to buy, and it will change the face of our country's industrial real estate markets because placement will become even more specific. Metro areas will become part of Corporate America's supply chain future—or be left out.

Where We Were

In the last 30 years, there were two great periods of industrial real estate building, and both times the market eventually collapsed coincidental to drastic slowdowns in the economy.

The first lengthy construction period, when new building was hitting record numbers almost every year—from a minimum of 120 million square feet to 185 million square feet annually—finally ended with the great real estate recession at the start of the 1990s, reports REIS Inc.

Recovery came relatively swiftly with the high-tech explosion that began in the mid-1990s, and REIS reports industrial completions were over 100 million square feet from 1996 to 2001. With the dot-com bust, new construction waned and it appeared the industrial market had finally learned its lesson as new construction remained moderate, no higher than 80 million square feet in 2006. REIS predicts the market will stay at this level through the early part of the next decade.

"The development cycle tends to be shorter for industrial, so it is a lot easier to turn the spigot on or off depending on how much money is flowing into new product," says ING's Copeland. "If you are building office or retail you need longer lead times to address leasing."

Part of the reason for the trend line of new building moderation was a market hangover of double-digit vacancies that lasted until 2004. Although by REIS's accounting, this vacancy never reached higher than 11 percent, remember even at that moderate level, stress begins to pervade this sector. (TWR incorporates a wider range of industrial buildings in its reporting, but even it showed the highest vacancy at 11.7 percent in 2003.) Since 2005, the vacancy rate in industrial has been under double digits according to both REIS and TWR and is expected to stay that way well into the next decade.

Bulking Up on Distribution

After a healthy 2007 in terms of investment volume—a record $46 billion as compared to $12 billion in 2002—Real Capital Analytics wasn't enthralled with the way 2008 began. Sales in February 2008 were off 50 percent from the year before and cap rates were rising. Although there were no distressed sales, Real Capital Analytics expected there might be some pressure to sell among the private equity funds, which had invested about $4 billion into the sector the year before. The problem for the private equity folks was that many of their deals were financed with relatively short-term debt and bridge loans.

Despite all those problems, the one bright spot on the horizon was distribution, or what Real Capital Analytics called, "big box warehouses."

In 2007, over 1,600 distribution facilities greater than 100,000 square feet exchanged hands, reported Real Capital, representing $29 billion of sales. Early in 2008, Real Capital observed, "While sales have recently declined due to a dearth of portfolio transactions, activity in this distribution niche has not witnessed the same decline as other property types."

Around the time the subprime markets were blowing up in the summer of 2007, ProLogis, a company that focuses extensively on distribution, formed a new North American property fund to acquire at the sale price of $1.85 billion a 25-million-square-foot portfolio of distribution space from DP Industrial, a joint venture between Dermody Properties and CalSTERS, the California State Teachers Retirement System.[2]

Dermody Properties develops about 3 million square feet of industrial product every year. Back in 2008, when I spoke to Michael Dermody, president and CEO of the company that bears his name, he wasn't expecting to slow down. "There are always changes in the supply chain," he said. "The shifts mean difference nuances for every real estate sector. But, underlying fundamentals don't change. Our plan is to be in good locations, with good infrastructure, near good crossroads and port locations."

Dermody is based in Reno and has an office in Harrisburg, Pennsylvania. Both are top 20 locations for warehouse/distribution facilities. "Out of Reno, you can serve the entire western United States, whereas Harrisburg is a good location to serve New Jersey and the Northeast," he says.

Michael Dermody obviously knows his product and target market and that's important because one of the key points going forward in regard to distribution facilities is that, as part of the corporate supply chain, where they are located is of particular importance. Generally, the new distribution facilities will be in limited locations, near ports, important interstate intersections, or rail hubs.

"We have an investment strategy where we invest in port proper-ties," says Charles Schreiber, chief executive officer of KBS Realty Advisors, one of the country's largest acquirers of commercial real estate and manager of KBS Real Estate Investment Trust, a publicly registered, nontraded REIT. "Our industrial strategy is to buy land or buildings that we think will handle the volume of products imported via ships."

KBS, along with two other investors—Hackman Capital Partners and Calare Properties—formed a joint venture to buy in 2007 the Equity Industrial Partners Corp. portfolio of mostly warehouse/distribution properties for $516 million. The 11.4-million-square-foot portfolio con-sisted of 31 buildings and some raw land in seven states.

"Locations of the properties were primary hubs for distribu-tion," Schreiber explains. "These are not manufacturing buildings, these are distribution buildings. As we track population growth, dis-tribution of products to retail stores becomes more important."

Although there were a handful of smaller manufacturing and flex structures scattered in the Equity Industrial Partners portfo-lio, the main target was the distribution, of which no building was smaller than 200,000 square feet. On the opposite end of the size spectrum, one of the largest buildings totaled 1.1 million square feet, and the week I interviewed Schreiber, he was telling me that the tenant in that building wanted KBS to build another 400,000 square feet next door and raise the roof eight feet. It was currently 24 feet high, but the tenants wanted a 32 foot clear height.

That's the other trend line in the new-generation distribution buildings: They are larger, higher, and come with the latest tech-nology in stacking, distribution, and fire suppression systems. Distribution buildings are becoming so cavernous there is now an emphasis on cubic space as opposed to square footage.

"The logistics business changes the requirements for space users," adds ING's Copeland. "Ten years ago, a big box was consid-ered 300,000 to 400,000 square feet. Today, a big box is 800,000 to 1 million square feet. The bigger box gets used by third-party logis-tics firms and major retailers."

Copeland explains, "You hear a lot about just-in-time inventory and common sense will tell you it is working, but after 9-11 and the longshoremen's strike at the port of Los Angeles/Long Beach in 2002, which caused a logjam at other ports, the people managing supply chains realized they cannot afford to have empty shelves so they are inventorying more to guard against a break in the supply chain."

Just about every major retailer and distributor in the United States has been shifting to a regional instead of a local model and that requires these huge centers of distribution that can handle a number of states. Retailers have been consolidating. Instead of having a center on the outskirts of six cities in six states in the Midwest, they are opting to close all those down and open a giant distribution facility that can service all those cities from one location.

The question for Corporate America's executives is How do I move product through the distribution channels faster and more efficiently, and the answer, says McKiernan, is that companies have gone to fewer and fewer distribution centers. "The typical model now is, rather than have 20 or 30 warehouses around the country, consolidate down to 2 or 4 massive distribution centers."

The advantages are a significant savings in costs as companies use a smaller footprint, choosing perhaps 1 million square feet in the center of the United States and then distributing from there around the country. "The technology and systems to do that, for example, to identify by bar code each individual item, has allowed companies to do this," says McKiernan.

In Phoenix, where I'm located, a number of retailers in recent years have been building 500,000-, even 1-million-square foot facilities that can handle Arizona, Southern California, Nevada, and New Mexico.

In the Southwest, the Dallas-Fort Worth area, which sits along Interstate 35 (the NAFTA Highway) that goes into Mexico (and north to Canada) has been greatly benefiting as a regional hub. Duke Realty Corp. built a 1.1-million-square-foot spec building in Grand Prairie, near Arlington, that it boasts was one of the biggest speculative distribution buildings in Texas. That's just part of the 18.6 million square feet of new warehouse/distribution space that was expected to come online in 2008, up 12 percent from the year before.[3]

Further north, Kansas City pretty much sat out the industrial development boom of the last decade, but in 2004, the tide turned, as the metro area suddenly was put on the map as a good location for distribution. Kansas City also sits on Interstate 35, but more importantly four major rail lines run through the city, and two rail firms, BNSF Railways and Kansas City Southern Railways, are teaming up with developers to create 1,000-acre intermodal parks.

From 2005 through 2007, companies that expanded distribution in the Kansas city area included: Musician's Friend, over 700,000 square feet; Pacific Sunwear, over 400,000 square feet; Kimberly-Clark, 450,000 square feet; and Corporate Express, 250,000 square feet.[4]

Before 2004, Kansas City was a local, sometimes regional, distribution market; now it's a local, regional, and national distribution market.

"It used to be you could count the number of transactions over 100,000 square feet on two hands in a given year," says Kevin Wilkerson, president of NAI Capital Realty in Kansas City, "but those deals have increased significantly in recent years."

Why Kansas City? Imported goods come into the U.S. ports and receiving companies want their distribution facilities nearby. However, there is not a lot of room left near Los Angeles/Long Beach or Newark, New Jersey, for new facilities, especially those around 1 million square feet, so ancillary locations, such as the Inland Empire (Riverside/San Bernadino) in Califorinia, and Harrisburg, Pennsylvania, grew in importance.

Containers, however, don't have to be broken down near ports. They can simply be taken from the ships and put on rail cars (rails have a significant cost advantage over trucking, especially with today's higher fuel costs), so the railroad companies have begun to create inland ports, or vast intermodal centers.

"Basically, the big 40-foot containers are off-loaded from the ships to the rail line and they are not being opened until they get to these huge distribution centers, where the goods are disseminated for short-haul, or one-day trucking," explains Cushman & Wakefield's McKiernan. "These distribution centers are at intermodal parks, which can be considered inland ports. There are a couple on the West Coast, two in Chicago, one in Houston, and now they are building two in Kansas City."

"We are in the middle of a huge structural change in the industrial warehouse arena where every major corporation needs a brand-new facility," says Dan Fasulo, managing director of research at Real Capital Analytics, the New York-based research company. "They need bigger floor plates, higher ceilings, new rack systems. The demand has not slowed for warehouse space."

Sounds terrific—yet, it really isn't.

The principal issue unfolding here is that most cities will *not* benefit from Corporate America's rationalization of supply chains.

The winners are already in place, and the losers hope for a trickle-down effect. Real Capital reports the two biggest big box warehouse locations are Los Angeles (Los Angeles/Long Beach is the country's largest port on the West Coast) and Chicago (the largest rail center in the country). In descending order are NYC Metro (numerous locales to serve the Northeast), Atlanta (rail and road hub in the Southeast), Dallas (rail and road hub for the Southwest), and then SF Metro, DC Metro, Seattle, Boston, and South Florida (the last three being port cities). Real Capital counts just 25 major big box warehouse markets in the country, and that might be stretching the label.

Clearly, in the coming decade there will be winners and losers in the distribution facility raffle. Some cities in the top 25 will lose status while other locations deemed less favorable might actually gain revised stature.

Most cities will still get their fair share of smaller distribution centers, but the revolution of Corporate America's supply chain will centralize the big facilities in a small number of select locations.

Where We Are Headed

During the current economic slowdown, absorption of new space will severely decline, but pundits expect American industry to start gobbling more space at an increasing level. As soon as the economy gets righted, REIS predicts net absorption will get stronger and that by 2012 the country will start showing numbers not seen since 1997 when the United States was in the midst of a high-tech explosion.

A very positive sign that the industrial real estate market maintains stability even in tough times can be ascertained from average national rental rates. REIS shows that rates have been steadily climbing since 2002 without a down year. TWR, using a different grouping of industrial buildings, reports rental rates dropped slightly in 2003. In 2008, when the year began in the throes of a credit crunch and slowing economy, REIS and TWR were estimating no growth and a slight improvement in rental rates.

"In the early 2000 period, which was the last downturn in the industrial market, from a tenant standpoint we didn't have a lot of companies going out of business or giving back space. In fact, our lease rates were strong," says Copeland.

Industrial tends to withstand market downturns a little better as cash flow issues are less pronounced, Copeland adds. Also, there is not much capital required to retrofit an industrial building that is vacated at least as compared to an office or retail property.

As for pure distribution space, the news is generally tepid in the face of the country's financial problems and economic malaise.

Most other property sectors reported extremely good years for new construction and/or investment in 2007, but most of the activity came in the first six months of the year before the subprime mortgage crisis blossomed full flower during the summer. ProLogis, an industrial real estate investment trust, which calls itself the world's largest owner, manager, and developer of distribution facilities, released in spring 2008 a couple of reports on bulk distribution facilities. The big surprise was that new starts in the prior year amounted to 145 million square feet with more space (79 million square feet) coming in the second half of 2007 than the first. In addition, net absorption in the second half of 2007 was virtually unchanged from the first half.[5]

Through the beginning of 2008, the bulk distribution market in the United States remained "surprisingly strong," commented Leonard Sahling, ProLogis' first vice president of research. "As the U.S. economy teeters on the brink of a cyclical inflection point, the overall fundamentals for those property leasing markets are in better shape than they have been prior to the past few down cycles."[6]

By midyear, the outlook dimmed considerably. In 2008, U.S. retail sales, which had been weak, spiraled downward and a number of retailers such as Sharper Image and Steve and Barry's failed. Many of the survivors, from Starbucks to Home Depot, were cutting back on growth plans. All this affects the industrial market, because retail companies are the major tenants.

Remember the Dermody buyout? When Lehman Brothers filed for Chapter 11 in September 2008, the deal came back into the harsh light of the business press. It turns out Lehman was ProLogis' partner on the deal and to get the deal done quickly, it supplied the debt financing and 80 percent of the equity. It's estimated that by September 2008, the value of the portfolio dropped 15 percent, for two reasons: The deal was done just as the credit squeeze began, and the retail industry has been in a steady decline ever since.

It's tough to remain optimistic for the remainder of this decade when a large part of the tenant base for industrial enters difficult economic times. No one really wants to see 1 million square feet of space under one roof sit vacant.

Bonus Box

Flex Space

After a healthy year for flex space in 2007, Real Capital Analytics noticed a dramatic change in the outlook for this light industrial product. By early 2008, flex properties were undergoing the sharpest increase in cap rates and price declines since the onset of the credit crunch.

The problem, says Dan Fasulo, managing director of research at Real Capital Analytics, the New York-based research company, has to do with the "perceived quality of the tenants" who usually take this kind of space. Flex properties have a large share of start-ups and other small companies whose credit is difficult to evaluate. "Flex is usually occupied by small, hopefully fast-growing firms that need less than 100,000 square feet," explains Fasulo. "The tenant is a little shakier."

The definition of flex space is a bit imprecise. Some of the major brokerage firms combine it with R&D as one category and list it as R&D/Flex. Overall, flex space is considered light manufacturing with a small part of the floor plan devoted to office.

"Flex space or R&D/Flex is tricky to categorize," says Matthew Anderson, a principal in Foresight Analytics LLC, a provider of real estate market data. "It tends to be similar in rent to Class B office space, and it does blend office with a small warehouse in the back."

The heyday of flex space was back in the dot-com days, and today a lot of this kind of industrial product can still be seen around San Jose and Northern California, Boston, Austin, and other technology nodes. In these areas, prices for flex space held through 2007. The most expensive cities to acquire flex space at the peak of the market, according to Real Capital, were three California cities: Los Angeles at $251 a square foot; San Jose, $202; and San Diego, $195. In comparison, at peak, Boston flex space was pricing at $95 a square foot.

R&D/Flex has not been as strong as distribution in terms of the number of properties being built, says Luciana Suran, an economist with CBRE/Torto Wheaton Research, but there are still a few markets where R&D/Flex is a big draw like San Jose, Boston, and Austin.

Looking over a Grubb & Ellis report on the Austin industrial market in early 2008, the city does appear to be an anomaly as its hottest industrial sector continues to be R&D/Flex where the largest absorption gains occurred. As 2008 began, warehouse/distribution showed negative absorption, but Austin is not a distribution type city. It is more

Continued

(Continued)

of a high-tech center, which is why absorption was strong and rents increased in flex space. Nevertheless, even in a city like Austin, where R&D/Flex should be healthy, it is not really. The vacancy rate in Austin for this type of light industrial space was 16.6 percent, highest of any industrial category and much higher than the 10.3 percent overall industrial vacancy rate for the city.

Flex space always has its moments—then just as quickly loses momentum. The demand for R&D/Flex was off the charts during the dot-com boom only to fall apart with the high-tech bust at the turn of the millennium. Then came the 9-11 recession and as Fasulo notes, "There was almost no interest in these types of assets. When the economy came back around in 2005, demand and pricing started creeping back up, especially in the three hotbeds of flex space: San Jose, Boston, and Austin."

The Equity Industrial Partners Corp.'s portfolio of industrial buildings consisted mostly of distribution space, but there were four large Massachusetts properties listed as flex/warehouse facilities—an usual notation. Chuck Schreiber, CEO of KBS Real Estate Investment Trust, indicated he was going to keep those flex/warehouse buildings although when Equity Industrial Partners was acquired, the objective was the distribution/warehouse properties.

The R&D/Flex market began to get real hot again in early 2007 only to see interest disappear after the onset of the credit crunch later in the year.

"The technology sector is the classic tenant for R&D/Flex, so the outlook for the product depends on the outlook for high tech," says Anderson. "The technology sector has always been cyclical, which makes R&D/Flex cyclical. The ups and downs won't be as big moving forward as they have been in the past."

Over the last couple of quarters there just hasn't been a lot of flex properties being developed, Michael McKiernan, Cushman & Wakefield's executive managing director for industrial brokerage, told me in the second quarter of 2008. "It's a niche market. Today, the majority of that space is being used as one-story office for R&D purposes or assembly. It's not really what's going on in the industrial sector."

The cap rate rise for flex space indicates a certain nervousness about those tenants that occupy space. In times of turmoil, everyone wants to populate their buildings with AAA-credit tenants. Entrepreneurial companies, which often turn to flex space, are a long way down the credit continuum. The length and depth of the economic slowdown will determine whether flex or, as the case may be, R&D/ Flex, makes another one of its miraculously rapid leaps to boomtown.

Manufacturing

In the spring of 2008, my local newspaper, the *Arizona Republic*, ran a story in its business section about the manufacturing boom in a central Mexico city I never heard of. The place was called Queretaro and what prompted industrial expansion there was the presence of a number of U.S. and Canadian aerospace companies.

Among the firms taking advantage of the low wages were General Electric (built a research center there for designing jet engines) and Bombardier Inc. (runs a huge factory making jet parts such as tail sections). Other aerospace firms in Mexico include MD Helicopters manufacturing fuselages near Monterrey and Goodrich Corp., building a 350,000-square-foot factory in Mexicali to construct engine nacelles for the Boeing 787 Dreamliner.[7]

According to the *Arizona Republic*, Mexico's aerospace-related exports more than tripled since 2004, from $146.2 million to $683.2 million.[8]

All this got me to thinking about William Sanders, the great real estate entrepreneur I profiled in *Maverick Real Estate Investing*. In 2003, Sanders founded Verde Realty because he believed there was a megashift in manufacturing jobs from the Midwest and Northeast to the Southwest United States and Mexico, stretching from California to Texas and blossoming on both sides of the border. Verde Realty began buying industrial land in and around the twin cities of El Paso and Juarez, Mexico. His company didn't distinguish between opportunities on either side of the border.

I interviewed Sanders back in 2005, and it appears he was right on the button about the trend line in manufacturing.

About the same time the *Arizona Republic* was running the story about Queretaro, the *Wall Street Journal* showcased on its front page a story about the shift from fading factory jobs to booming health care employment. Alongside this article was an interesting map that highlighted areas where manufacturing jobs were declining or growing. Across the whole country, the number of places where manufacturing jobs were up numbered just 10 tiny locations, one of which was right on the U.S.-Mexico border where California bumps Arizona.

I compared that map with another from the Economic Policy Institute that highlighted "manufacturing job loss as a share of total employment." This was a state-by-state map and the only five states increasing manufacturing jobs as compared to total employment

Continued

(Continued)

were those with low populations: Alaska, Utah, Nevada, North Dakota, and South Dakota. However, of the states with flat to small declines were three on the Mexican border: Arizona, New Mexico, and Texas.

Just as an example of the variety of activity along the border, toward the end of 2007, BASF Corp. opened two new manufacturing plants in Freeport, Texas, for the production of polyamide 6 (nylon) and super-absorbent polymers (SAPs). The polyamide production line replaced a facility in North Carolina.[9]

The Carolinas along with Michigan have lost the largest share of manufacturing jobs since 2001.[10]

Michigan has lost thousands of automobile manufacturing jobs. Where did those jobs go? A lot of them went to places like Mexicali, just south of the U.S. border. Mexico, in fact, exports $42 billion in cars and auto parts every year.[11]

When I asked Sanders about the types of facilities down his way, Sanders told me, "In U.S. industrial parks, most of the buildings are for bulk distribution, but down here only about 20 percent fall into that category. The rest are incubators, supplier, manufacturing, and customer service centers."[12]

There will always be situational requests for manufacturing structures in most U.S. cities, but the real expansion for industrial plants will be in the regions on both sides of the U.S./Mexico border.

CHAPTER THREE

THE RETAIL REAL ESTATE

Mixed cart of goodies as new shopping center, mall outlook turns sour; Sweeter future at start of next decade

The sudden onslaught of the credit crisis after the collapse of the subprime residential market in 2007 claimed a couple of early victims. The most prominent, of course, was Bear Stearns & Co. Inc. But even before the big Wall Street firm was forced to sell itself to JPMorgan Chase & Co., the earliest casualty was a major real estate company—Centro Properties Group of Melbourne, Australia.

Although not well known in the United States, the Australian company was one of the largest owners of shopping centers in this country, with 700 U.S. shopping malls sitting in its portfolio. It attained such prominence in the usual manner: It bought big. Early in 2007, Centro acquired New Plan Excel Realty Trust for $3.4 billion.[1]

The problem for Centro wasn't the real estate, it was the manner in which the New Plan Excel acquisition was done: Centro borrowed most of the capital using shorter-term debt to finance long-term investments. With cheap money still available, Centro did what most real estate investors were doing. They took advantage of the availability of short-term capital with the certainty that it could find long-term financing to take out the always expensive short-term debt. When the credit crisis ensued, liquidity dried up and Centro's big bet fell apart.

As I was writing this chapter, Centro was still looking for a way out of the morass and was in danger of default.

Centro's problem was one of financing, not one of real estate and shouldn't be reflective of the retail real estate sector. Yet by 2008, retail real estate, once wildly popular with institutional investors, had lost its luster. As with other real estate sectors, retail real estate enjoyed a glorious 2007 right up until the fourth quarter.

According to Real Capital Analytics data, a record $74 billion of retail properties changed hands in 2007, which was up significantly from the $54 billion the year before. Again, as with other asset classes, almost all of that was done in the first three quarters. Real Capital Analytics dryly noted, "The credit crunch caused sales of significant retail properties to fall by 31 percent to $10.1 billion in the fourth quarter."[2]

Even though retail real estate investments did collapse, the sector still maintains a lot of fans. If the near-term prospects for office or industrial properties seem fairly clear, the road ahead for retail real estate remains murky. Some analytics and investors still like the sector, but others are frantically waving the caution flag.

The problem with retail real estate is that it is probably the most idiosyncratic of all the major real estate asset classes and that's because it has the important third-party factor—the retailer that leases the space—that makes it different from other real estate.

Location as always is a primary ingredient to a successful shopping center concept. Sitting in second position and almost as important is the retailer that will take up the space. Although the retailer may be a national company, it has to be successful on a very local level. Third, this is a sector that gets sharply separated into categories. At the top of the heap are the shopping malls and to some extent the new life-style centers (outdoor versions of the old shopping malls); and then come shopping centers, neighborhood shopping plazas often anchored by supermarkets and/or drugstores and basic strip centers; finally, there are the single-tenant stores that are acquired by investors and leased back to the retailer.

In an office building if a tenant departs, the landlord goes about finding another tenant. In a shopping center, the loss of a tenant can get complicated. If a key retailer leaves, other retail tenants may follow. Some may even have contractual arrangements noting that if a certain anchor tenant departs, it can also do so without legal redress.

"If you have a neighborhood shopping center anchored by a supermarket and that supermarket leaves, you will have a half dozen other tenants that will have the right to leave because it is written in their lease," says Jim Koury, managing director of retail investment sales at Jones Lang LaSalle in Chicago. "The other tenants have that right because they rely on the supermarket to draw in income."

In shopping centers (especially malls), if a tenant leaves, it is not enough just to find any old tenant to fill the space; the next tenant needs to be at the same price-point level. A simple example: If you own a shopping center with upscale retailers and a high-priced restaurant closes, McDonald's might be willing to pay the rent and move in, but a fast-food restaurant can ruin the mix of shops.

Another nightmare scenario for a manager of an upscale retail project: A tenant files bankruptcy protection and sells the lease in the bankruptcy proceedings to another retailer or restaurant that is not wanted in the shopping center.

"Institutional investors looked at retail as having unique characteristics," notes Sam Davis, senior managing director and head of real estate with Allstate Corp. in Northbrook, Illinois. "There are aspects to retail that many institutional investors feel comfortable with and others do not. It is very management intensive. Secondly, the success of retail real estate owners and managers has a lot to do with their relationships to retailers. There is a whole investor theme around owners and operators of retailers and only doing business with those companies that have a long list of relationships with retail tenant companies."

"The other caution about retail," Davis adds, "is that the downside of a failed retail center is often greater than the downside of office or industrial properties. You can have a loan out or an equity investment in the best grocery-anchored retail center in the best part of town and if a new retail center gets built a mile down the road, it could mean the end of your center. Performance can drop dramatically. Think of how many empty retail centers you drive past."

Finally, on the shopping mall end of the business, there has been so much consolidation of ownership that most of the major shopping malls are now in the portfolios of just a handful of companies. With consolidation has come a certain amount of power. A company like Simon Property Group Inc. of Indianapolis, the number one shopping mall owner in the country, can now say to a retailer: If you want to be in my Miami mall, then you also have to be in my Anchorage mall. To investors all seems right with the world, because they view a particular shopping mall property, which has a Gap, Abercrombie & Fitch, Victoria's Secret—all the usual suspects—as a good investment. Figuring this potential investment has the crème de la crème of tenants, the investors acquire or refinance the property, not realizing that some stores are only there because they were strong-armed by the mall owner, and the first chance the retailers get to be gone, that store will close down.

"We are starting to see a trend where some prominent retailers can no longer afford to be all over the place," notes Chauncey Mayfield, president and chief executive officer of MayfieldGentry Realty Advisors Inc., a Detroit-based investment advisor.

The outlook for retail real estate gets clouded by the outlook for retailers, which in turn, is based on the economy. Depending on what you read, the United States slipped into a recession or near recession in 2008. Unemployment rose and consumer spending declined. Much of this had to do with the problems in the residential sector, where homeowners were losing their residences to default or having to pay a higher percentage of their income to maintain themselves in their homes.

Since retail is tied to the housing market and consumer spending, retail real estate ends up being one of the more vulnerable sectors of the commercial property markets.[3]

In April 2008, the *Wall Street Journal* spotlighted the real estate market for Denver, which boasted a relatively stable economy. Office vacancies were down, lease rates up, industrial vacancies down, lease rates up. Yet, the median home sale price declined from $292,134 in February 2006 to $278,871 in February 2007. Correspondingly, retail vacancies were on the rise and lease rates were falling.[4]

"We are seeing a decline in consumer spending, which obviously has an immediate impact on retail," says Dan Ansell, a partner at Greenberg Taurig LLP and chairman of its real estate operations department. "Retailers are in a bad situation because consumer spending is down and some stores are not generating enough in revenue. Also, because of the credit crunch, they cannot borrow money to weather out the storm. It is a matter of time as to how long they can last under these circumstances."

When consumers stop spending, retailers suffer. Already Pacific Sunwear of California Inc. announced it was closing its 154-store Demo division; jewelry retailer Zale Corp. was shuttering 100 stores; Footlocker will be locking the doors on about 400 outlets over a two-year period; and Wilsons The Leather Experts is truncating 160 of its outlets. Even Starbucks announced store closings. In 2007, retailers closed 4,603 locations; the International Council of Shopping Centers expected nearly 5,800 closings in 2008.[5]

"If we have a mild recession, experts believe retailers will suffer a 2 percent loss in 2008 with a recovery in 2009," Ansell says. "If the recession is severe, some experts predict retailers could lose 6 percent this year and recovery won't come until 2011 or later."

For property owners, the good thing about investing in retail real estate is that leases are long term, usually 5 to 10 years—with options. This is normally a good deal for retailers as well because if rents in the shopping center rise, their position doesn't change as they are set with a long-term lease. However, if markets go south, the long-term lease becomes a shackle.

"In retail real estate, rents are so high in comparison to other types of commercial real estate that retailers roll the dice fairly early on a long-term lease," says Ansell. "Unfortunately, even if the income stream of the store declines, the rents due under the lease remain the same. The retailer cannot get out of that lease unless it renegotiates or takes some kind of bankruptcy position."

Where We Were

Jones Lang LaSalles' Koury remembers going to his first International Council of Shopping Centers convention in 1991 and seeing a banner over the stage that read STAY ALIVE UNTIL 1995.

The convention was in the worst year of a very deep real estate recession that began late in the 1980s. Retail real estate was not only overbuilt but much of it was in the hands of private investors who had gotten into the market relatively easily with loan-to-values ranging from 75 to 90 percent. By 1991, many of these properties were underwater.

The 1995 prediction was pretty darned accurate, Koury notes, because it took that long for not only retail but other commercial real estate markets to stabilize and begin to attract institutional investors. At first, the institutional players were drawn to the office and industrial markets as they were fairly easy to figure out. Retail took a bit of time, but when it eventually showed up on the radar of institutional buyers, the shopping spree began.

"There was a stretch in the late 1990s to early 2000s, where not a heck of a lot of retail was getting built," says Davis. "What I mean by that is, the average of new supply being added to the market nationally tended to be under control in most markets. New supply was fairly well constrained, so when the economy started picking up in 2002, retail rental rates started climbing at a faster pace than the other major property types."

Giving a big boost to retail was the failure of negative expectations. At the end of the 1990s, the prevailing opinion was that traditional retailing was going to disappear with the advent of the Internet. In some regard it was a shunned asset class, that is until everyone realized that brick and mortar retail wasn't disappearing but was thriving.

"One could make the argument that the Internet actually drove more activity to brick and mortar retail," says Dan Fasulo, managing director of research at Real Capital Analytics, the New York-based research company. "Whereas there was this under-weighting of retail in investors' portfolios, suddenly we saw a wave of investment."

After the dot-com bust when a flood of capital washed into commercial real estate investments, retail was one of the dominant property types. Until 2007, retail accounted for 26 percent of all commercial real estate acquisitions, says Fasulo. In 2007, it slipped to 17 percent.

In a very short period of time after the millennium, retail real estate was bolstered by two separate investment waves. Around 2004, early investors started to realize some fairly amazing gains on their investments, so an intense sell-off period followed. However, those profits were reinvested back into retail because of 1031 exchange rules (exchange of certain types of property can defer capital gains or losses). New capital was washing into retail real state at the same time existing real estate profits were being reinvested, and it really created a kind of investment tsunami.

According to Real Capital Analytics data, in 2001 $11.8 million of retail real estate changed hands; total investment dollars rose quickly to $59 million in 2004. That market stalled for two years until 2007, when it busted loose (at least until the fourth quarter of 2007) and a record $74 million in deals were done.[6]

As the economy goes, so goes the retail investment market. Just a few years back when the economy was strong, bolstered by very low interest rates, consumers felt they had more disposable income and spent more. Retailers responded to demand by expanding everywhere. They wanted to be in more locations, open more and more stores. The frenzy was so out of control, that at one point in the early 2000s, retailer real estate departments were signing leases for space sight unseen. All they knew was that they had to have more space so many new stores would be ready to go over the next 12 months.

Any retailer expanding today is definitely being more selective in placement. Even mass retailers such as the Gap are rethinking their location strategies. Does it want to be in the high-priced mall or would a better location be across the street in the outdoor shopping center?

Where We Are Today

In regard to retail real estate, the foot hit the brakes immediately. Optimism over rent growth and extremely favorable financing caused average prices to surge early in 2007, but by the end of the year, optimism gave way to recession fears and financing disappeared, says Fasulo.

In the second quarter 2007, the average price of strip centers peaked at $184 a square foot. By the beginning of 2008, that average price had tumbled to $156 a square foot. In 2002, cap rates on closed deals stood at nearly 10 percent; by early 2007 they had fallen to almost 6.5 percent. By 2008, the cap rate was ticking upward again, already passing 7 percent.

One odd phenomenon of the braking retail market was that property owners tried to quickly get out of the market before it all turned to garbage. In the fourth quarter, properties put on the market spiked by 50 percent, reports Real Capital Analytics. Most were withdrawn after failing to achieve price expectations. The good news, says Fasulo, is that sellers are not at the moment under pressure to sell or accept steep discounts and that has kept prices from falling further.

Follow the Rooftops

As for bad news, there's plenty of it. The biggest problem has to do with new product. As the housing boom exploded over the past decade, huge new developments grew like dandelions on the periphery of metropolitan areas. Retail developers, following the new markets, staked out vacant weeded lots, paid top dollar for the land, and started building knowing that whole new neighborhoods were going up all around.

This was the follow-the-rooftops concept, and it worked as long as residential developers kept building—and they did until 2006 when the strategy fell apart. Retail developers who tried to get out ahead of the new developments got very lonely, very suddenly.

"Over the past few years, retail construction has become an issue," says Sam Chandon, chief economist and senior vice president of REIS Inc., the New York real estate research firm. "There is a lot more space coming online than we have seen in a decade. A lot of this construction activity was planned over the last couple of years when we were in the housing boom."

Here's what happened. Smaller grocery-anchored shopping centers were built alongside or even colocated with housing developments because if you were going to build on the periphery, those folks who wanted to live out there—wherever it was—also needed amenities such as local shopping. And here's where we are today. "Vacancy rates for those new spaces in strip malls are on the order of 32 percent," says Chandon. "They are having a hard time filling those spaces because the housing developments are not filling their spaces."

Since 2005, developers produced more retail space than any other commercial real estate category, adds Greenberg Taurig's Ansell. "Some research suggests if trends continue, the present demand justifies less than 50 percent of that new space." That's an optimistic view.

In 2007, developers built 144 million square feet of space in the top 54 U.S. markets and had another 131 million square feet in the pipeline for 2008, reported Property & Portfolio Research Inc, a Boston research firm. They also calculate that demand justified 36 percent of the new space built in 2007 and just 15.7 percent of the space scheduled for 2008.[7]

If there is a bright spot in all of this, it's that many projects in the pipeline will never get built.

"The main engine of finance for a large portion of construction projects has been the commercial mortgage-backed securities market," notes Christopher Volk, president and chief operating officer of Spirit Finance Corp., a Scottsdale, Arizona, firm that provides sale and/or leaseback financing to owners of single-tenant real estate. "For practical purposes that market doesn't exist at the moment because there are no buyers for conduit paper. Projects that don't have firm commitments won't get done unless money can be found outside the conduit market such as with insurance companies or certain commercial banks."

Early in 2008, the CMBS market wasn't totally dead, but it was barely breathing. Through the first three months of the year, U.S. CMBS issuance totaled $6.9 billion, about one-tenth of the activity in the first three months of 2007.

Where We Are Headed

Other issues also litter the retail scene.

"Conventional wisdom tells me people still need to go to the grocery store for food or the pharmacy to fill a prescription. But they might be looking for cheaper alternatives," says Chandon. "Consumers might decide to go to a Wal-Mart or Costco, and that puts more downward pressure on shopping centers."

Retail construction consistently followed the consumption boom as consumers, from the start of the millennium through 2006, were growing their spending faster than their income and were doing so by extracting home equity. Two years later, the consumer household stands heavily in debt and the capacity to grow spending will be severely limited in the years ahead.

A more serious concern, Chandon adds, is with the regional shopping malls, which benefited from the consumption boom, especially with the expansion of prime retailers. By 2008, those same prime retailers were looking very overstored. As a result even mall anchors like Macy's were trimming stores.

"This is the beginning of what will become a bigger problem in the next few years," observes Chandon, "as there are some weak retailers that are really overextended in terms of how profitable individual stores are."

Chandon pretty much hit the nail on the head because the day I was writing this chapter I was perusing the *Wall Street Journal,* which ran a story with the headline "Retailers' Woes Weigh on Mall Owners." After listing a number of mall denizens that were closing stores, the article noted, new construction would raise the total amount of retail space in 2008 by 3.5 percent in the top 54 U.S. markets. Unfortunately, with retail sales slowing with the economy, demand will justify only one-third of that new space.[8]

Even the strongest stores won't be able to expand as they would like. Not because of the market, but due to a lack of liquidity in the financing markets.

Early in 2008, Spirit Finance called upon several major retailers including dollar shops and drugstores that bragged about their aggressive growth strategies. "They have slowed down because the take-out financing that was once available to developers is not as strong as it once was," says Volk. "In addition, a lot of these businesses cannot pass through inherently high rates or even higher rents because the margins are not there to support the numbers."

What doesn't bode well for bottom-line fundamentals is a sudden trend line that would be more accommodating to tenants. Mall landlords, scrambling to keep tenants, have resorted to the usual ploys, forgoing rent increases, covering more tenant costs in customizing space, and allowing struggling retailers to move into smaller, cheaper space.[9]

"What we hear from the retailers is that they are willing to renew leases but only if the rents are kept the same; otherwise they will move out," says Mayfield. "That is what they are putting on the table in order to renew."

"Rent growth will be anemic over the next couple years," affirms Chandon.

Fundamentals are weakening for the retail real estate sector and that will continue at least until late 2009, says Chandon. For regional malls, the outlook is a little nastier than with community shopping centers, although it won't be so apparent because the problem won't be so much of increasing vacancies but softness in rental rates.

Neighborhood and community shopping center fundamentals won't weaken too much. That's mostly because it is a relatively stable product (except in new development areas). Vacancy rates on a national level may rise to 8 percent, and that's not really too bad considering that back in 2000 vacancy rates were only 6.4 percent. Not a lot of change.

That's why investors still like the product. For Allstate, grocery-anchored neighborhood retail centers, usually in the 80,000- to 150,000-square-foot range, remain the bread and butter of its retail investments. "These kinds of centers continue to perform through economic cycles better than other specialty retail such as strip centers or stand-alone retail," says Davis. "Drug- and grocery-anchored centers have been a good place to be over the last 20 to 30 years. In a bad recession, they will have some problems but they usually are strong performers and I still believe in them."

Davis isn't just hanging fire with anchored shopping centers, he's also hedging his bets. "I tend to do most of my business in the 30 largest metro areas." His rationale is that the largest metro areas offer a scale of business; depth of market; liquidity from other lenders and equity investors; and a measure of protection from new developments, which in smaller markets can throw the supply and demand equation out of balance.

Sure there was a problem with retail chasing rooftops, explains Richard Moore, a managing director with RBC Capital Markets in Cleveland, but it's an endemic situation, not anything new. It takes a certain number of years to construct a retail center because of entitlements, planning with a city, and finding tenants, so retail developers have to look ahead to see where the population centers are going to be.

"They can't just look at where they currently are," he says. "Obviously, some population centers were being built with the anticipation that we needed more housing, which we didn't, and now those home builders have fallen on hard times. The shopping centers that were associated with these new developments are no longer needed."

Locally, this type of situation has meant overbuilding, yet in general, there really has not been a fundamental amount of over-building—certainly not like at the end of the 1980s.

"Unlike any other property type where all you need is the bank and the landlord to have a property, in retail you need the bank, a landlord, and a major tenant or a bank won't do a loan," Moore explains. The major tenants, such as a Wal-Mart, have a pretty good idea of where they should be. Nordstrom's knows where it should be. So does Target and grocery stores. The tenant situation is a form of checks and balances."

Moore ignores the spec development that is built in hopes a retailer will eventually come along, because banks really don't like to finance those kinds of projects anymore.

Also taking an optimistic view of retail is Robert Bach, chief economist and senior vice president at Grubb & Ellis Co. "If you are looking at the neighborhood center that was built on the fringe in anticipation of more rooftops and then housing development stopped midstream, that is only one story," he says. "However, if you look at places where the trade area is already built out and there is not a lot of vacant land around, those existing centers should do well. Fortress malls (market dominant) with some of the best tenants will do well."

Bach's outlook: In the short term there is considerable risk in the retail real estate sector, but in the long run, retail will do well.

Not everyone is so sanguine about retail real estate.

MayfieldGentry Realty advises institutional investors on real estate, and it is currently raising the white flag. "We have taken ourselves out of the game on retail," Mayfield says.

One of the markets Mayfield once assiduously followed was the grocery-anchored shopping center and after being positive on this asset for a long time, he shifted negative and it was for a solid but unusual reason. He observed that most of the top 10 grocers that anchored these neighborhood shopping centers just a decade ago were no longer around. Consolidation and Wal-Mart took their toll on supermarkets. The market for anchors had gotten a whole lot smaller, which meant more neighborhood shopping centers were planned than there were stores to anchor them.

The second reason why Mayfield turned against retail has to do with the economy. A lot of newer centers targeted a more upper-class clientele. However, with the economy slumping, he perceived a shift by consumers to discount centers. His best example is the Fort Lauderdale market, where in recent years the Galleria Mall experienced foot traffic decline by 20 percent, but Sawgrass Mills, an outlet mall, saw foot traffic taper off by only 5 to 10 percent.

"Consumers will go to the discount store to stretch their dollars," says Mayfield.

At some point in the future after all the unsold real estate has gone to the discount bin, Mayfield will start shopping for bargains.

Beginning in the mid-2000s, says Mayfield, acquisition prices of retail real estate bore no relationship to underlying fundamentals.

The fund managers that dived into retail real estate didn't necessarily care because they had a 7- to 10-year horizon before having to sell and it was believed the markets would look better in the future.

That's not going to happen.

These funds generally will have to choose one of two options: Either they go back to investors and beg for an extension before they have to liquidate or they are going to have to liquidate on schedule at a substantial discount.

There is a third option, which Mayfield expects to see kick in. Fund managers will begin marketing pools of assets, essentially mixing "dogs and cows,"—a great retail center in the District of Columbia and money loser in Florida. While selling pools lessen the impact to investors, it is an indicator as to just how bad some individual investments have become.

Already in 2008, several large shopping center REITs began organizing ways to identify and buy out distressed private developers in the retail real estate market.

Let the sales begin.

Bonus Box

The Lowly Strip Center

The world of retail seems to get more magnificent every year. Neighborhood shopping centers are being turned into designer destinations; lifestyle retail parks picturesquely replicate urban shopping experiences; and even the malls keep getting redeveloped and reconfigured into grander and grander meccas.

Somewhere, further away from all that shopping grandeur, one can still find that most basic of all retail experiences: the strip center. Because they are often old and abused, sometimes new but half-empty, one would think the strip center is nothing more than a retailing dinosaur.

I'm here to say that is not true, and I can make that assertion with a degree of certainty. In Mesa, Arizona, where I reside, one of the state's most successful owners and managers of retail real estate continues to develop strip centers as well as neighborhood shopping centers.

Michael A. Pollack Real Estate Investments owns and operates about 100 different projects in Arizona, and about 65 to 70 percent

Continued

(*Continued*)

are strictly retail. "We don't do power centers, we don't do malls," says Pollack. "We have strip centers and we have nonanchored and grocery-anchored shopping centers."

Pollack thrives in this playing field because very early he recognized that the trend line for tenants continues to morph in odd ways. In fact, the strip center can barely be considered retail real estate anymore. Strip centers and unanchored shopping centers are dominated by small service businesses such as nail and hair salons, independent insurance agents, real estate agents, beauty supply wholesalers, pool supply outlets, mail shops, tax service firms, or in the only nod to modern retail, a simple chain eatery such as a Subway. Strip centers rarely house a true retailer.

As with other types of retail experiences, strip centers need to be well located, designed with enough parking, and be able to adequately showcase businesses that need to be there. Novice investors often think, "What can be an easier real estate play than a strip center?" They generally get it all wrong, says Pollack. They design them poorly with wrong ingress and egress, and they build without getting a sense of the competition. "You can only have so many nail and hair salons," he says.

Novice strip center investors have been known to follow the rooftops, trying to get ahead of new development. Pollack eschews this strategy. "I don't need a big swing in new housing or new growth to make my centers viable," he stresses. "I am an infill player, I don't pioneer areas. I don't go out to the next Casa Grande (Arizona) or the next Eloy (Arizona) or whatever is between any of that."

Pollack expects the general retail climate in Arizona will get worse before it gets better and that will affect tenants of not only shopping malls but strip centers as well. "Well-built, well-located centers will survive the turbulence," he says. "The ones that shouldn't have been built in the first place won't."

CHAPTER FOUR

THE MULTIFAMILY MARKET

Slowing but stable fundamentals ahead; Apartments will be the place to be in the next decade

Early in 2007, just a few months before the subprime mortgage blowup and subsequent credit crisis, two huge real estate deals were completed and announced. The first, the $39 billion purchase of Equity Office Properties by the Blackstone Group is the most well known. That's mostly because after the purchase, the Blackstone Group flipped billions of dollars worth of properties to help pay for the deal and the subsequent buyers such as Harry Macklowe were the ones caught holding the debt when financial markets suffered paralysis.

The second deal, the Lehman Brothers Holdings Inc./Tishman Speyer Properties purchase of multifamily real estate investment trust Archstone-Smith for $22 billion, has for the most part stayed below the financial press radar. This doesn't mean it was a success. In many, many ways, this deal was badly done.

The largest public to private merger and acquisition transaction done in the multifamily REIT sector came much too late in the cycle and wasn't well thought out in terms of recouping investment costs. The Blackstone deal was completed in February 2007. The Lehman/Tishman acquisition wasn't announced until May 2007 (just ahead of the subprime residential lending market collapse) and not completed until October 2007, when the black fog of the credit crisis was engulfing the land.

To Blackstone's favor, it was able to immediately flip out a substantial number of properties to secondary buyers. Lehman/Tishman professed an intention to sell properties, but they hadn't lined up enough buyers immediately. The economy had shifted much too quickly making it tougher to sell properties and since multifamily portfolios consist of smaller assets, a whole lot more individual deals needed to be done to recoup any significant amount of capital. Finally, the cost of the deal was so pricey that rent from all of Archstone's apartments wasn't enough to cover the $16 billion in debt placed on the company after the acquisition.[1]

Yet, for all that, it was assumed the Lehman/Tishman was a good acquisition. Why? Since it disappeared from view, one could guess there were no subsequent problems and therefore nothing for the press to write about. And second, it occurred in the multifamily sector (rental apartments, not condos), pretty much the Rodney Dangerfield of real asset classes. Multifamily plods along with little drama, low risk, and moderate returns.

"There's lower volatility in multifamily than you might see in hotels, offices, and retail," observes Peter Donovan, a senior managing director and head of the multifamily transaction sector for CB Richard Ellis.

Tishman Speyer is a private company so it doesn't have to report whether the Archstone deal was salutary or disastrous. Lehman, on the other hand, was publicly traded before the market forced it to file for bankruptcy in September 2008 and as the financial press began to parse its financial reportings that year, the light started to shine on the Archstone deal and what could be seen wasn't very pretty. Lehman held about $4.5 billion of Archstone's noninvestment grade debt and equity, all of which the company reported in spring 2008 were being carried "materially below par."[2]

Part of the financing package to buy Archstone consisted of $4.6 billion in bridge equity loans, which lenders planned to sell to other investors. That didn't happen because in 2007 and 2008, commercial real estate values were dropping like faulty building cranes in New York City. As to selling individual properties, even well into 2008 buyers hadn't materialized because they were waiting for prices to drop even more.[3]

For this chapter, I gave a call to Matthew Lawton, senior managing director of the Chicago office of Holliday Fenoglio Fowler LP (HFF) and head of the company's National Multi-Family Group, and asked if he was working on any Archstone properties. He responded: "A lot of Archstone properties have come up for sale. Some have traded; some have not. The ones that are trading have done so below Archstone's expectations. I think it's safe to say that Tishman, Lehman, or anybody else would not do that deal today at that price."

Finally, I was able to confer with the always frank Richard Campo, chairman and chief executive officer of another multifamily REIT, Camden Property Trust. When I caught up with him, he told me that just the week before, he had dinner with one of the key Archstone people. "Archstone has a great management team and great assets in great locations," Campo said, "but the banks are going to lose billions of dollars on Archstone."

Where We Were

Okay, so we do get some drama in the multifamily markets; it just doesn't happen very often. The last time was back in the 1980s when tax-driven deals drove multifamily production into overdrive and new units were coming into the market at a 500,000 to 600,000 clip, much more than the market could handle. Those numbers included all things multifamily, even condominiums and affordable housing, but those two components were very small then. When the real estate markets fell into a severe recession at the start of the 1990s, multifamily was ripe for disaster with much more supply in the market than demand.

Once the tax equation was taken out of the real estate markets and foreclosed properties were remarketed, multifamily settled into a decade and a half of relative consistency, "We have stayed at the better part of 300,000 (new units) for the past 10 years or longer," says Donovan.

Even though the 1990s was a decade of recovery and stabilization in multifamily, underneath the numbers an important cultural shift occurred that subtly began to change the face of the industry.

"In the 1990s, the Generation X people started coming into the market, and while there were fewer of them as compared to the baby boomer generation, there was a lifestyle change as many became renters by choice. Rental was often considered the step prior to homeownership," explains Greg Willet, vice president of research and analysis for M/PF Yieldstar.

"One result of the cultural change was that developers began building more upscale product, and rents climbed in many markets to a level equal to what a mortgage would be in a starter home. There were two parts to this movement," Willet continues. "First, much of the new development occurred in the suburbs where huge job centers were evolving, and then the concept of new urbanism began evolving with people wanting to move back into the cities."

While there has been a lot written about homeownership, the increase in renter households over the past decades has actually been very dramatic. According to Gleb Nechayev, vice president and senior economist at CBRE/Torto Wheaton Research, from 1965 to 1995, renter household percentages climbed from 61 percent in 1965 to 67.5 percent in 1995 before hitting a lengthy plateau (about the time interest rates began to fall and the movement to homeownership accelerated).

Although from 1995 to 2005 the percentage of renter households didn't change, what did change dramatically was the expansion of a category Nechayev calls "professionally managed apartments."

"There are over 35 million renters in the United States, more than half of them living in single-family homes, houses with two to four units in structure, and mobile homes. Professionally managed apartments—properties with five or more units in structure—capture only about 45 percent of the total rental demand nationally," Nechayev remarks. "These two markets are very distinct and saw rather different trends during the recent homeownership boom. The demand for professionally managed apartments expanded by 1.6 million units between 1995 and 2005, while the demand for other types of rental housing contracted by 2.8 million over the same period."[4]

Although the decade-long expansion of multifamily was straight upward, there were a few speed bumps along the trajectory.

Multifamily performance surfs the economic waves, but there are two theories on this. In effect neither played out smoothly at the turn of the millennium and that could give us some insight how multifamily will play out in the years ahead. The end of the last century brought with it the dot-com technology bust, which pushed the country into a mild recession that was prolonged by the September 11, 2001, terrorist attacks.

The first theory of multifamily says that when the economy slows, rental housing also moderates because when people are out of jobs they tend to save money on housing by doubling up in residences or moving back with family. There's another theory that apartments do well in a recession because people get more conservative and don't make investment commitments such as buying a new house.

Neither theory plays out too well because a third factor was introduced to the market early in the first decade: extremely low interest rates over a prolonged period of time.

"Class A multifamily usually has been bulletproof in an economic downturn," says Lisa Sarajian, managing director of real estate companies at Standard & Poor's. "But, right after the tech wreck and 9-11, high-end multifamily owners, operators, and REITs took it on the chin because they lost renters to home ownership (effects of aggressively promoted low interest loans). From 2001 to 2006, the multifamily sector materially underperformed the other property classes."

In the first quarter 2001, multifamily national vacancy rates stood at 4.1 percent and then climbed steadily until peaking at 6.8 percent in fourth quarter 2004, reports Nechayev. Those are fairly conservative numbers because other researchers show vacancies passed 7 percent in 2003 and 2004. Meanwhile, again according to CBRE, average national rents peaked at $1,040 in fourth quarter 2001, and we didn't see those numbers again until first quarter 2004.

Despite the low interest rate/single-family bubble and condominium pandemonium, the multifamily market continued to strengthen until mid-year 2007, when the subprime markets imploded.

Where We Are Today

Like all asset classes, multifamily performance varies extensively from market to market, so even though some Texas cities have barely noticed any change in fundamentals, most of Florida has been a disaster. Unfortunately, that won't change anytime soon because all those busted condo projects will end up as rentals at some point in the future. "The softest rent growth is mostly in

Florida and the cities of Las Vegas and Detroit," observes George Skoufis with S&P's Real Estate Companies Group. "In mid-year 2008, some cities such as Palm Beach, Phoenix, and Houston were sitting on average vacancies over 8 percent."

That's the odd thing about multifamily: At vacancy rates over 7 percent, that market begins to stress. In the office sector, an average vacancy rate of 7 percent is considered golden.

Sure, there's currently a weaker economy and excess single-family houses and condominiums are turning into rentals, but multifamily trudges along. Vacancy rates are slowly edging up, expecting to reach the mid 6 percent range by 2009 and 2010, says Skoufis. Meanwhile, average national rents are still rising, albeit at a slower pace than just a few years before. Back in 2004 and 2005, average national rents were climbing at a 5 to 6 percent pace; at the end of the decade, expansion fell into the 3 percent range—about the level of inflation.

"Supply and demand are still relatively decent," Skoufis says. "There's a bit of excess supply, but demand is still robust even with the job losses the country has been experiencing."

As the first decade headed toward a close, the market was weak but not far from equilibrium. Somehow, one expected more, a kind of Hulk-like invincibility from multifamily. With the single-family residential market all but dead, millions of likely buyers were supposed to pack up their belongings and head to apartments.

"A misconception," says Nechayev.

"The homeownership rate has dwindled while broader rental demand expanded," says Nechayev, "but apartment demand is tied to the economy and jobs so if the broader housing market goes through a severe correction as it is experiencing, it affects the broader economy and jobs. Also, falling home prices affect rent growth; those things are very much tied together."

In a period of rapidly falling home prices, rental rates don't dramatically rise. It does not work that way because rental is basically a substitute for a mortgage; apartments and homes are substitutes for each other. If home prices drop, rents don't rise that much.

If this sounds like economist-talk, it's not. Richard Moore, a REIT analyst for RBC Capital Markets argues the same point, but from a market perspective. He calls the single-family/apartment balance a double-edged sword.

"As the price of single-family housing rose sharply, it also made renting more attractive because houses were getting too expensive," he explains. "Demand for rental space grew and occupancy climbed. As a result, the prices of multifamily properties climbed."

Rental housing tracks for-sale housing, but in the middle of the first decade of the new century, things got a bit out of whack. Housing prices were rising faster than apartment rents; consequently, the cost to buy rose faster than apartment building prices. This dynamic couldn't hold and in fact it didn't: The single-family housing market collapsed.

As home prices came down, this began to affect the rental market. Homes that used to cost, for example, $2,000 a month in mortgage, could be bought for a $1,200 or $1,400 mortgage. That will have an impact on the rental market, where rents were already $1,200 to $1,400. Indeed, apartment prices are falling and cap rates rising—more so than any other property type.

"Nevertheless," Moore says, "even with prices coming down for properties and cap rates rising, there has not been a lot of pressure on earnings for the major owners and operators of apartments. Rents seem to be hanging in there. Rental growth has been expanding at the rate of inflation. Sure, it used to be faster, but the world hasn't come to an end and there is still demand for rental property. That will keep prices stable to some extent."

CBRE shows rent growth slowly climbed from 2006 to 2008, rising from a national average of $1,100 in the fourth quarter 2005 to $1,199 in the first quarter 2008. Average national vacancies drifted downward to the 4 percent level in the third quarter 2006 and have been slowly climbing ever since, hitting 5.5 percent in the first quarter 2008.

S&P's Skoufis says average national vacancy rates will continue to climb until 2010, but shouldn't get much worse than 6.6 percent. Over that period, rent growth will hover in the mid 3 percent range.

Investment Interest in the Asset Class

Remember, the Archstone-Smith deal? In mid-2008, the *Wall Street Journal* ran a story on one of the buyers that carried this headline, "Lehman's Property Bets Are Coming Back to Bite," and it noted,

"Lehman's strategy has been to sell individual Archstone apartment complexes to pay down debt. But so far, sales have proven difficult because buyers are waiting for prices to fall further."[5]

Sales of multifamily properties for 2008 will end up at about the same level as 2003 or 2004, observes Dan Fasulo, managing director of research at Real Capital Analytics, a New York-based research firm. Even though that's about half the total pricing volume of 2007, Fasulo says other asset classes such as office and retail dropped even more.

"Multifamily has probably held up the best of all property types," says Fasulo.

That's because multifamily held an ace in the hole: government-sponsored agencies, better known by the acronym GSAs.

"The GSAs still provide liquidity on the debt side," says Fasulo. "You can still get competitive mortgage rates from the Fannie Mae and Freddie Mac. Also, the FHA (Federal Housing Administration) has stepped up its lending for smaller types of properties. We have not seen the same type of correction in cap rates for apartments as we have seen for other asset classes."

In September 2008, Fannie Mae and Freddie Mac were taken over by the federal government, but were still functioning under their prior mandate. The GSA boosted a faltering transactional market by providing some liquidity. It's just not enough considering everything else that is happening around the markets, from a weak economy to lack of credit to a sense that things will get worse in the apartment sector.

For example, most players realize that a shadow market of condominiums and single-family residences has been and will continue to impinge on the apartment sector. Except for Florida, where the shadow market is huge, no one is really sure how this will affect other markets.

"If you or I, or even the banks, are sitting on an empty condominium or home, and cannot sell, what do you do with those properties but rent them?" asks Moore. "And typically you rent them at below market rates because you are not in the business. You are not trying to maximize rents. You look at the going rental rates and say, 'I will rent mine cheaper' to entice renters and that puts pressure on existing rental properties."

As I'm writing this chapter, the last reportable quarter on multifamily transactions was first quarter 2008. As compared to the fourth quarter 2007, transaction sales were down 67.5 percent, but that is probably an unfair comparison because the $22 billion Archstone-Smith sale closed in the fourth quarter 2007. Still, as compared to fourth quarter 2007, transaction volume was off 41.1 percent. In addition, the market value of investment-grade apartments in the National Council of Real Estate Investment Fiduciaries, or NCREIF, database rose by 0.2 percent from the previous quarter and by 4.9 percent from the same quarter the year before, the smallest quarter-to-quarter increase since the first quarter 2002.[6]

In 2001, $17 billion worth of multifamily properties changed hands. By 2004, that number jumped to $37 billion and continued to rise until a peak of $70 billion in 2007, reports Real Capital Analytics. For 2008, Fasulo didn't expect transactional volume in multifamily to exceed the levels of 2002 or 2003, which was $18 billion and $24 billion, respectively.

This is not to say there aren't buyers out there.

Chauncey Mayfield, president and chief executive officer of MayfieldGentry Realty Advisors Inc., a Detroit-based investment advisor, likes the multifamily asset and is pursuing a number of deals. "Multifamily investments offer consistent cash flow, so when the real estate markets are down, as they are now, returns are stable," he says. "If the market improves, then you can do a conversion to condo or sell out. It's almost like a hedge in a down market that allows you to capitalize on a market upswing."

One of the markets Mayfield has been looking to buy in is Florida, but it's still a minefield. "One of the sellers I was speaking with had a 150-unit development with an initial projected retail price of $750,000 to $800,000 a unit. They would sell to me at $300,000 a unit," Mayfield explains. "The problem is, I cannot get rents to even support $300,000 a unit."

In order to make a deal work in South Florida, Mayfield estimates he has to buy under $150,000 a unit.

Sellers are not desperate enough to sell, says Mayfield, and the reason is the difference between this real estate recession and the one 20 years ago. Back then, the banks moved quickly to retake failed properties. Today, banks are reluctant to foreclose and put so many bad loans on their books. As a result, sellers are not yet feeling enough pressure to unload busted properties so quickly.

The market for multifamily appears to have bifurcated between smaller purchases—$20 million to $50 million properties—and large projects, usually the assets of choice for larger institutional investors. Regional companies have been active picking up the smaller projects.[7] This is especially so in secondary and tertiary markets because so many institutional buyers have bailed out and put those properties up for sale.

Where We Are Headed

The one data point that gives us some direction as to where the multifamily market is headed going into the next decade is new construction.

"The capital markets are so disruptive in terms of construction money and equity that development deals are generally unachievable," observes CBRE's Donovan. "People are looking for 20 to 25 percent equity return, difficult if not impossible to achieve considering the cost of construction. Add to the fact that you probably have to put 30 to 35 percent into a transaction and you end up with everything going the wrong way."

"There will be a lot less new construction," Donovan adds, "and the impact will be felt starting in 2009."

I'll let someone working in the heart of the industry, Camden's number one man, Campo, explain it all. "Total completions (multifamily) over the last 10 years have been about 300,000 units, but if you take out for-sale and subsidized projects like retirement homes, you get down to 180,000 rentals. In 2008, that number could go down to 170,000 units and then drop considerably, so by 2010 and 2011 we could be at 20-year lows, or just 100,000 units being delivered."

He adds, "If you look at a company like Trammel Crow, they predicted 15,000 starts in 2008, but their best-case scenario is 6,000 to 7,000 starts. When you talk to the other major builders such as JPI or Fairfield, their starts are off by 50 percent as well. In 2010 and 2011, you could have some of the lowest annual completion numbers in recent history."

What has happened is a lack of overlap. From the time a multifamily project is conceived and goes through all the design, financing, permitting, and local review, it could be two years before the start of construction. Even with the slowing economy in 2008 and 2009, there were a lot of projects that had gotten under way or were committed to in the previous two to three years that were coming to completion.

"In some cities there is a spike in deliveries just because the deal was in place," says M/PF YieldStar's Vice President Gregory Willet. "Even if it doesn't make sense to start building, you do so, because you don't want to be in a position of going back and having to renegotiate the money again."

Starting in 2007, but clearly in 2008, financing dried up, which means that around 2010 there will be a lack of new development. "A new number of projects were started and will deliver in 2009," says Willet. "Starting in 2010 deliveries will come down dramatically and this could last through 2012."

The scenario for multifamily will probably unfold in this manner. Due to the weak economy, shadow market, and continued new delivery of product, occupancies will remain soft and therefore problematic in selected markets like Florida but nothing too severe for the rest of the nation. At the same time rental growth will range from nil to moderate.

Even if the current capital malaise hangs about longer than expected, by the early years of the next decade the economy should be on the mend. It will happen at a fortuitous time for multifamily. Demographically, the eco-boomers, children of the baby boomers, a large cohort, will be entering the rental market in a major way. In addition, strong immigration is expected to continue.

"In the next decade, demand for multifamily rentals should be very strong," says Campo, "and we will be going into the decade with low supply."

Taking all that into account, the multifamily sector should experience a boom period not seen since the 1980s.

"Starting in 2012 or 2013, it will be a landlord's market, not a tenant's market," HFF's Lawton predicts.

At the start of the next decade, when the market is not delivering much new product, the economy should be creating a decent number of jobs, says Willet. "By that time we will have worked through this current excess of inventory in all housing products, and the demographics are going to be pouring huge numbers into the rental marketplace. After 2010 to 2012, it will be an incredible performance period for this sector."

"Before anyone gets too excited," Willet warns, "we still have to wade through the end of this decade to get there. It's hard to judge how much multifamily markets will soften over the next year and a half."

Bonus Box

Locations for Knowledge Workers

When I was setting up my interview with Jim Koury of Jones Lang LaSalle (JLL) for Chapter 3 on retail, Craig Bloomfield, the company's vice president of public relations, suggested I also talk to Richard McBlaine, JLL's president of strategic consulting, as he had some interesting theories on how companies locate new operations.

There was something intriguing about the suggestion, so I told Bloomfield to go ahead and set up a telephone interview. And then I sat on the transcript for a while wondering where it would fit into this book. As I finished up this chapter, I returned to the transcript and realized McBlaine's thesis was very important.

Distilled into one sentence, this is what McBlaine said: "Whereas in the past, white-collar workers gravitated to cities where the jobs were, now companies are gravitating to cities where they can find these workers."

Bloomfield wrote me a corollary: "As baby boomers retire, there are fewer college graduates replacing them, yet the demand for these knowledge workers is increasing dramatically. Recent grads increasingly choose the place they want to live and look for a job, and companies are basing their expansion decisions on those choices."

But, before writing this chapter, I checked in with Jay Biggins, executive managing director of Biggins Lacy Shapiro & Co., a specialty site selection and incentives advisory firm. "Yes," he affirms in direct response to my questions, "we can confirm the trend."

Now this site location thesis is based on the concept of the *knowledge worker,* a term that has recently come into vogue, but, in fact, has been around for a long time. The phrase is attributed to Peter Drucker, who had been writing about knowledge work and knowledge workers since the 1950s. The knowledge worker is one who works primarily with information.

As America continues to shift to a more service-oriented economy, as opposed to manufacturing based, most employees are now, in some regard, knowledge workers.

How this affects site selection, says Biggins, is mostly based on two factors: (1) a scarcity of labor, partly, as McBlaine intimated, due to the next cohort coming into the marketplace, which is smaller than the one (baby boomer generation) leaving; and (2) the increased need for an educated worker (education requirements thin out the supply of workers).

"These trends will force companies to be more selective in site selection," he says. "Instead of companies deciding to put operations where they want to for various other reasons and assume the workforce will come to them, it pushes companies to consider where they can compete for the best workforce."

McBlaine explains it this way: "Big companies that need specialized skills in engineering, science, or even finance are finding it important for them to consider where the knowledge workers, who they are trying to attract, live. Ten years ago, it was a little more of 'build it and they will come.'"

Here's an obvious example. If you want to attract good financial services workers, then the place to establish this kind of operations center is in and around New York, where there is not only a concentration of such workers but also a location that continues to be Mecca for top talent in this sector.

High-tech and biotech have their own concentrations in places such as Northern California, San Diego, Seattle, Boston, and Austin. (There are still some companies such as Google Inc., based in Mountain View, California—in the heart of the Silicon Valley—that can get young knowledge workers to flock to it, but most companies, even IBM, are not in that position.)

This trend line to go where the workers want to be will have a positive effect on bigger cities, because if there is no other overweighting factor, companies will look at population density, knowing that in the mass of populace, they can probably find the knowledge workers they need. That would mean the older concept of creating new operations centers on the outskirts of a suburb holds less appeal. The new generation of knowledge workers has a tendency to want more urbanized living.

McBlaine, who lives in Chicago and loves his city, wonders how it will even be able to compete in the future. "We have a high quality of life here and real successes in attracting business, but we have had a net loss in terms of the number of Fortune 500 companies located here." The city did attract the Boeing Co., which moved its headquarters to Chicago from Seattle. That may say more about Seattle's ability to attract knowledge workers rather than those in the technology industries.

"Chicago has some advantages because of the universities here," says McBlaine. "Young people come to the universities and stay after graduation, but Chicago is in a race against other places that are trying to attract knowledge workers and provide a high quality of life."

Continued

(Continued)

Other older cities such as Pittsburgh, as an example, also boast quality universities, but it has had a problem in keeping its graduates. I live in the Phoenix area and the local economists also talk about the issue of keeping the graduates of Arizona State University in the region after they get their diploma.

My question to both McBlaine and Biggins was "Are we then creating have and have-not cities?"

McBlaine felt this was a concern, but Biggins claims there is a moderating factor that will help other cities. For the past decade, a slew of knowledge worker jobs in the business processing sector—accounting, programming, administrative services, and call center personnel—were outsourced to low-wage countries such as India. Biggins feels that that trend line has run its course and many of those jobs will come back to places like Phoenix.

"The herd instinct that fostered the massive shift in asset and employment to venues overseas is almost done," he says. "If you are the next company into Vietnam, you may be too late. The pro forma cost savings that motivated that move are not now being realized. In fact, on an all-in, true-cost basis, the savings are increasingly seen as not worth the move. Some of those jobs may come back."

McBlaine adds, "There are certain kinds of back-office jobs or non-client facing jobs that require knowledge workers who absolutely can be based in more efficient cost locations in the United States than the Northeast or California."

PART

II

OTHER ISSUES IN COMMERCIAL REAL ESTATE

CHAPTER FIVE

SUSTAINABILITY

Don't look now, but the future has arrived; Commercial real estate takes the LEED

When explaining the theme of this book to sources, I often used the word *megatrends,* which was a term made popular by John Naisbitt in his book by the same name. Upon invoking the word, most people immediately understood the intent of my book-writing attempt, but one very sharp real estate investor suggested to me the word had a very precise meaning: A *megatrend* was a future trend as opposed to one that we might be presently living through.

Frankly, I wasn't sure that was what Naisbitt had in mind when he wrote his transformative tome back in 1982. But if my source was accurate in his supposition, then I was already behind the scope of my book with this chapter on real estate and sustainability, because Green initiatives in regard to new commercial real estate development had in just a few years become the norm.

"I cannot imagine anyone starting a Class A building today in any major urban area that would not be LEED- (Leadership in Energy and Environmental Design) certified," exclaimed Dan Rashin, senior vice president of Hines Interests, an international real estate firm based in Houston. "I cannot remember the last announcement that I saw on a major building that did not include LEED."

Even though Rashin was essentially correct, Green programs in real estate are, nevertheless, fairly new and still evolving. Today's emphasis on certain standards or ratings may shift in the years ahead. And there is the whole question as to what happens with existing buildings.

Where We Are Today

Back in 1998, Hines Interests formed a joint venture with the California Public Employees Retirement System (CalPERS) to develop and acquire office buildings. Over the years, the $275 million (can be leveraged up to 75 percent) fund shifted emphasis and decided to no longer do ground-up development, says Rashin. One of its last projects, however, was an Atlanta office building called 1180 Peachtree. The time was still early in this century and despite the novelty of something called LEED-certified, the fund decided the concept was environmentally promising and 1180 Peachtree became the first LEED Silver (a rating) building in the world.

In 2006, the 41-story 1180 Peachtree sold for $400 a square foot, which was a record price in Atlanta. Sure, at the time, office building deals all across the nation were setting records, but, as Rashin notes, "The question that emerged after the deal was, did investors care about the building being Green?"

There was no definitive answer, but soon afterward CalPERS, a state pension fund ranked as the largest in the country, decided to go Green in regard to its core real estate investment practices. That meant not just talking about being environmentally aware but actually doing something about it. Its two key actions were (1) investing $100 million in a Green Fund with the Hines Group to focus on investing in buildings certified under the LEED program and (2) adopting back in 2004 an Energy Efficiency Plan for its core real estate properties. In fact, CalPERS set an energy reduction level of 20 percent over a five-year period.

When CalPERS, one of the largest real estate investors in the country, went Green, the tipping point for sustainability in commercial real estate was passed.

A Green building today meets one or both of two standards. First, there's the Environmental Protection Agency's Energy Star® program, which measures a building's energy performance. The higher the Energy Star score, the more efficient the building. The Energy Star scale runs from 1 to 100, and a score of 75 and above qualifies for the Energy Star label. Coincidental to the EPA's rating system, a group called the U.S. Green Building Council (USGBC) promulgates the LEED® Green Building Rating System™, which has become the national benchmark for green construction, design, and maintenance.[1]

The Energy Star system, with its calibrated continuum, is easy to understand. The LEED program is more variegated, as it has formed LEED ratings sytems for new construction, existing buildings, and tenant space build out. Instead of using numbers, the progression of LEED ratings starts at Certified and then moves upward to Silver, Gold, and at the top of the environmental heap, Platinum. (These levels are attained by accumulating points through the process of meeting certain baselines in sustainability, water efficiency, energy and atmosphere, materials and resources, indoor environmental quality, and innovation.)

Although it seems like it's been around forever, the LEED rating system was only formulated in this century.

"LEED was developed and came online in 2000," says Jason Hartke, manager of the state and local advocacy for the USGBC. "To illustrate the type of growth we are seeing, we now (spring 2008) have over 1,300 certified Green LEED projects and nearly 10,000 in the pipeline as registered projects."

Hartke gushes, "It has really been amazing growth. In 2006 we had about $150 million worth of construction registering with LEED every business day and today that figure is $450 million."

Oddly, the great leap forward of LEEDs was not so much fueled by the private sector, but from local governments. A number of cities, such as Boston, started passing Green building policies around 2003 and 2004; and by 2005 there was a huge spike in governmental activities. Initially, the early municipal policies simply required that any new city building be constructed Green and then came a host of incentives for other developers such as grants, tax credits, and reduced zoning and permit fees. In early 2008, about 120 localities around the country had some form of Green legislation.

San Francisco adopted a requirement in 2004 that all municipal buildings need to meet LEED Silver performance standards. "That was fairly early," says Mark Palmer, San Francisco's Municipal Green

Building Coordinator. "When we did that, there was only a handful of cities that had done that before we did. More have jumped on the bandwagon since."

Since then the city has been trying to up the Green ante. In 2008, San Francisco Mayor Gavin Newsom's Green Building Task Force proposed an ordinance that would require new commercial construction of more than 5,000 square feet, residential buildings above 75 feet, and renovations to buildings of more than 25,000 square feet to be LEED Gold certified by 2012.[2]

"We are crafting an ordinance that would affect the private sector," says Palmer, "and we are pretty much out in front on that issue. Only one or two other municipalities have done anything in regard to the private sector."

Like the flu bug, Green fever is very communicable.

In 2007, I profiled for *Urban Land* magazine what was going to be the Greenest office structure in America: the new $178 million, 254,000-square-foot corporate headquarters building for San Francisco's Public Utilities Commission (PUC).

Anthony Irons, PUC's deputy general manager, boasted to me that the new PUC headquarters would be "the most energy-efficient office building developed in an urban setting in the United States." I didn't doubt him because the unique office tower would not only be using proven conservation techniques but on the roof of the building there was going to be an unusual and unique technology: horizontal wind turbines to generate electricity.

I wrote at the time: "The picture most people have of wind-powered turbines are the very tall towers with tremendous propellers that are often found on wind farms covering hundreds of acres. That wouldn't quite work in an urban location, so the new PUC headquarters building will use corkscrew-like wind turbines that can be stacked vertically. The machines will be hidden behind glass walls so as not to be seen from the street and roofed over with photovoltaic cells. In effect, a kind of wind tunnel populated by turbines will be created."

Another PUC headquarters concept that has generated outside interest is the use of solar cells. Gridlike photovoltaic panels that harvest sunlight will be embedded in the outer walls, particularly the south-facing façade, and be arranged as part of the 15,000-square-foot cap on the rooftop's mechanical systems.

In the point system for the LEED Green Building Rating System, there is a section called Energy & Atmosphere, and structures are rated on four criteria: establish energy efficiency and system performance, optimize energy efficiency, encourage renewable and alternative energy sources, and support ozone protection protocols.

Truthfully, most of the current generation of Green buildings don't go nearly as far as what PUC is attempting. But I was curious as to what extent new buildings would use advanced alternative energy sources such as solar power, which in one form or another has been around, well, forever. So, I checked in with a San Francisco company called Recurrent Energy, which according to its web site, brings solar electricity to mainstream markets by building, owning, and operating solar power systems for owners of large property portfolios.

At the beginning of 2007, when Recurrent Energy would contact potential customers, "it took several weeks just for them to find someone in the organization for us to interface with," laughs Matt Garlinghouse, a Recurrent Energy co-founder and vice president of energy services. In just one year, the world had changed. "Now when we contact firms, they already have someone responsible for sustainability or real energy, depending on the size of the portfolio," Garlinghouse adds. "They now have someone responsible for evaluating Energy Star and LEED certification. They have someone who can interface with companies like ours."

Since solar has a long investment recapture period, the idea behind Recurrent is that they will own and operate the solar generating systems, making the decision to use solar much more amenable to property owners. Besides, of course, transforming rooftops into a value-generating asset.

A couple of trend lines are intersecting. First and foremost is the continued rise in electricity costs. Then there is the improved solar technology. And the final factor in the mix is the demand from tenants for sustainability features. "A year ago, companies had no idea who they even should be talking to about sustainability," says Garlinghouse. "Now they have Green initiatives and are looking for solutions."

On the East Coast, the go-to company for going Green is a New York firm called GreenOrder, which calls itself a sustainability marketing firm. It has worked with companies as diverse as General Electric, DuPont, and Starwood Hotels & Resorts Worldwide. It was, however, its work with a real estate company that helped change the thinking about Green in Manhattan. Silverstein Properties, the lease-holder of the World Trade Center, understood that after 9-11, a new development on the World Trade Center site had to be inspiring and built for the ages. One of the first attributes Silverstein Properties recognized that would give long-term value was to be Green. Around 2003–2004, GreenOrder began working with Silverstein to achieve that goal.

"Silverstein along with a few other New York property developers really led the way in the early 2000s to start thinking Green," says Nicholas Moore Eisenberger, a GreenOrder managing principal. "After starting from a position of near zero, now two to three years later there has been a dramatic revolution in the real estate industry about sustainability. In New York, there is now an ordinance that says that any building receiving a degree of financing from the city has to be Green certified." He asserts, "In Manhattan, there is not a high-profile, Class A office tower that will be built that won't be Green."

Value Proposition

It would be nice to say the commercial real estate industry has quickly taken up the banner of sustainability because they are great people and care about the environment. This might be true, but the rapid transition to a Green world wouldn't have happened if there wasn't some value in doing so.

At first, it might have been a marketing ploy, a way to distinguish one building from another, but as the corporate world, too, wanted to be on the side of angels, it quickly became apparent that Green was going to be an issue that would attract major-league tenants. Second, at this point in the evolution of Green buildings, there is a value differentiation between the new Green office towers and older buildings that are not Green, although the older buildings might still be Class A space. And, finally, being effectively Green should mean there is an inherent cost savings to run the buildings—after all, the point is to diminish the usage of energy, water, and so on.

In 2007, the Tenant Rep Agency, LLC, in St. Louis decided to endorse and promote Green standards. That didn't mean the Tenant Rep Agency required its clients to accept LEED or Green standards, but it adopted the LEED standard as the official benchmark of good stewardship.

It has long been assumed the promotion of Green benefits or LEED certification construction was the exclusive venue of the real estate owner as promulgated through the developer or office manager. However, the Tenant Rep Agency felt that in many cases it was the tenant who provided the means by which landlords make their money, so it seemed perfectly logical that the tenant could drive home the Green ideal.

"In the large corporate world, there are two kinds of clients," avers Christopher Desloge, the Tenant Rep's chairman. "One is the corporate entity that is responding to its shareholders who want Green and want Green options in corporate policy, and the other is the tenant that approaches Green from a moral responsibility."

Since so much of the country's office market space predates the Green movement, there is a LEED for commercial interiors, the benchmark for tenant improvement. LEED-CI is charged with certifying high-performance Green interiors that are healthy, productive places; less costly to operate and maintain; and have a reduced environmental footprint.

LEED-CI means that one doesn't have to feel guilty about moving into a non-LEED-certified building. That's important because there exists plenty of Class C and Class B, plus most of the Class A space, that was constructed without a LEED designation.

In 2007, the global commercial real estate firm Studley Inc. worked with utility company Exelon Corp. on the construction of its 220,000-square-foot building in Chicago, which in early 2008 was the largest office building in the country to receive Platinum LEED status for commercial interior office space.[3]

Studley now has a Sustainable Real Estate Practice with its own LEED-accredited professionals. "We are offering a resource to all our brokers around the country, helping them when they have clients that are looking for Green in their space," says Olivia Millar, director of Studley Sustainability and Workplace Strategies.

Essentially, the service was created because of requests from clients, Millar says. "In 12 months' time, from 2007 to 2008, we have seen the trend move from just individual organizations that one would expect to be sustainable-sympathetic to a cross-section of industries, from law firms to charities to financial institutions."

TIAA-CREF's goal is to help those people in such diverse fields as academia, medicine, the cultural sector, and even research, plan and live in retirement. With over $435 billion in combined assets under management, the big New York-based pension plan serves 3.4 million active and retired employees of over 15,000 institutions. Parts of those investments reside in real estate. As can be expected, an organization as large as TIAA-CREF can boast considerable heft in its property portfolio, with $70 billion of direct and indirect investments.

In 2008, TIAA-CREF announced it was going to improve the energy efficiency of its real estate portfolio by 10 percent over the course of the following two years. With that, the organization began an energy benchmarking initiative across its 43 million square feet of office buildings and other properties, looking to identify opportunities to reduce energy consumption.

Asked about TIAA-CREF's direction in sustainability, Nicholas Stolatis, the pension plan's director of strategic initiatives, turned the question around: "How can any intelligent investor not pursue a Green policy?"

On a basic level, utilities represent a fairly significant part of operating expenses for an investment property. So, being able to control these expenses goes straight to the bottom line.

Green buildings can reduce energy costs by up to 30 percent with existing energy-efficient technology, notes the *CoStar Green Report*, published by CoStar Group, Inc., the Bethesda, Maryland, provider of information services to the commercial real estate industry. A study by McGraw-Hill found that by going Green, buildings would experience an average expected decrease in operating costs of 8 to 9 percent across the industry, a predicted average increase in value of around 7.5 percent, and average return on investment expected to rise 6.6 percent.[4]

Buildings considered inefficient by the Environmental Protection Agency spend $3.37 a square foot annually on energy. Most commercial buildings in this country are fairly efficient and spend $1.81 per square foot. However, an Energy Star building spends just $1.27 a square foot. An efficient 200,000-square-foot office tower will spend $674,000 a year on energy, whereas an Energy Star building of the same size will spend $254,000.[5]

One should just think of the word *Green* as meaning nothing more exotic than efficient operations, notes Stolatis. "There are so many compelling reasons for an owner of real estate to move forward and seek out opportunities to operate in a Green way."

A 2008 Jones Lang LaSalle–sponsored study reported most corporate chief financial officers believe sustainability can lead to cost savings and increased revenues.

"The question each of us should ask is whether we are taking an aggressive enough position, given the rapidly approaching tipping point of the (Green) issue," comments Lauralee Martin, JLL's global chief operating and financial officer.

Today's warehouse and distribution centers, for example, are often larger than 1 million square feet and run around the clock, so the better operating efficiency, the happier the tenants will be, suggests the *CoStar Green Report,* which added, "To be honest, the less (tenants) have to pay in utility costs, the more they can pay in rent."[6] Good news for commercial landlords.

Green buildings operate more efficiently and boast better fundamentals, highlights another CoStar Group research paper, which reported LEED buildings command rent premiums of $11.33 per square foot over their non-LEED peers and have 4.1 percent higher occupancy. Rental rates in Energy Star buildings represent a $2.40-per-square-foot premium over comparable non-Energy Star buildings and 3.6 percent higher occupancy.

"We have a very firm idea of what a LEED building looks like in terms of environmental benefits," says Hartke. "We are talking about a 40 percent reduction in water, 36 percent savings in energy, 70 percent reduction in solid wastes, and 40 percent reduction in carbon emissions."

It costs 2 percent more to build Green buildings, reports the USGBC, and on average the payback comes within the first 12 to 24 months because of cost savings. Over the life of a building, which conservatively can be just 20 years, the return grows to 10 percent.

Signaling institutional investors, CoStar declared a trend line had formed about the widening valuations between energy-efficient Green buildings and those that weren't. According to CoStar research, Energy Star buildings in 2008 were selling for an average of $61 per square foot more than peer group buildings, whereas LEED structures commanded a "remarkable" $171 more per square foot.

It's a stretch to rely on this purported trend line because energy-efficient buildings, especially LEED-certified structures, are relatively new and even if they weren't, "Green" would still trade at a premium compared to older buildings.

If we take the CoStar report at face value, then the real trend line going forward is the opportunity to play on the older, non-Green buildings. As Green designations become more important, the value of older buildings will deflate (comparatively). Opportunistic investors will acquire the older buildings at a discount, retrofit them with a sustainability infrastructure, and then put them back on the market with Green certification and a premium price.

This is a trend line that is just beginning to appear. "Honestly, we would view the differential between a Green and non-Green building as an opportunity," says TIAA-CREF's Stolakis. "We could acquire and then go in and implement whatever changes are needed. Make a capital investment to make the property more operationally efficient. The differential will flow to the bottom line and help increase the return on our investment."

Where We Are Headed

Situated at One Bryant Park in Manhattan, the Bank of America Tower has from day one of construction sought to be the first high-rise office building with a Platinum LEED designation.

Even before the end of construction on the new bank tower, Bank of America had already adopted what it called "aggressive" voluntary targets to reduce greenhouse gas emissions across the franchise by 2009 to 9 percent below 2004 levels. As part of that process, it will invest $1.4 billion to achieve LEED certification at all new construction and banking centers.[7]

To achieve Platinum status, Bank of America reports 50 percent of building materials come from within 500 miles of the site; uses daylight and automated, light-dimming window shades; subfloor air distribution allows for climate control at each workstation; and expected energy consumption will be 50 percent lower than a conventional office building.

The Bank of America Tower is the future in regard to sustainable buildings. Not because of its unique, energy saving features, but because the bank executives "aggressively" pursued the Platinum rating. As noted, LEED uses different rating levels. If as everyone in the industry suggests, at least in regard to office buildings, LEED universality is quickly being reached, then because the developers are so competitive, the next differentiator won't be Green or not-Green, but my LEED rating versus your LEED rating, my Platinum versus your Silver.

Prudential Real Estate Investors (PREI), a subsidiary of Newark-based Prudential Financial Inc., is one of the largest publicly owned property investors in the country. It operates in numerous ways, including working with a joint venture partner to create investment funds, which invest in existing buildings and new development.

When I spoke to J. Allen Smith, PREI's chief executive officer, his company was developing a $1.2 billion office building in mid-town Manhattan that will have LEED Gold status. "When we secured this site, we were not entirely clear what level of LEED certification we would go with," he says, "but it became obvious as we got into it, by the level of tenant demand, the incremental cost to make it LEED Gold certified instead of LEED Silver certified was insignificant, so we took the next step."

Office buildings are a visible example of how companies engage in the world. For tenants, if they can say they operate from a Green building, it's a good thing. Corporate executives want to be able to report to their employees and shareholders, "We are being Green. Even the buildings we occupy are Green."

What is going to happen, Smith speculates, is that employees, shareholders, and corporate executives will become more knowledge-able about the characteristics of a Green building and once that happens, they can be an even more demanding and discerning group. "It's a natural evolution," Smith continues. "As people become more astute consumers of space, they will say, it's great that this is a Green building, but I want a building that meets the LEED Gold standard (or Silver or Platinum) and I want these specific attributes."

LEED certification will become just a baseline designation.

Will LEED qualifications then become increasingly more demanding? I asked that of Hartke. The rating system continually improves and has gotten more stringent as time has gone by, he said. "The reality, however, is LEED is about leadership. We believe in the leadership model (not LEEDership model) to transform the market, so there are various levels of achievement. Today the number of Platinum buildings is not very high, certainly not to the point where we need to think it might be too easy."

Existing Buildings

Whereas Green has quickly penetrated the new construction market, especially for office buildings, our cities are filled with hundreds of millions of square feet of existing office space, some of which are in famous structures. Everything from the Bank of America building in San Francisco to the Sears Tower in Chicago and every building surrounding these iconic structures were built decades before the world decided to go Green.

"This is the 800-pound gorilla in the room," jokes Prudential's Smith. "Frankly, it's easy to do a new construction Green building, but if you look at the rate of new construction, you don't achieve meaningful penetration, especially when you are adding just 1 percent of new office stock a year."

This is where much of the sustainability activity will be in the coming years. All this older stock of space will need to be transitioned into Green space. Probably the alterations will not come from existing owners, but every time one of the buildings changes hands, Green renovations will be implemented. Actually, it's not much different from the current trend line. New owners generally upgrade the new additions to their portfolios; they modernize and beautify real estate investments to keep them current and competitive in the marketplace.

For example, investors, when they underwrite the acquisition of a 15-year-old office building, will be factoring into their considerations the cost of retrofitting the building and bringing it up to the minimum standard Green buildings. "Tenants will demand it," says Smith. "Clearly, tenant demand has been a key reason for the adoption of Green standards by developers. Where a building falls in terms of its Greenness is a source of quality differentiation in the market; the degree with which a building has been retrofitted with Green features will also serve to denote quality differentiation."

"There is a tremendous amount of opportunity in 'Greening' existing building stocks," explains USGBC's Hartke.

Indeed, the USGBC does have a LEED certification for existing building operation and maintenance and in 2008 it went through an extensive revision—also, a name change.

The good news for much of the existing building stock is that being Green can be easy, comments *Buildings Magazine*, which further noted: "While LEED for new construction is about design and construction, LEED for existing buildings is about operations and maintenance. Too many people don't realize this very important and opportunistic distinction. In fact, because there is market misunderstanding of what makes an existing building Green, the USGBC changed the name of LEED for Existing Buildings to LEED for Existing Buildings: Operations & Maintenance."[8]

The idea behind the name change was to emphasize operations and maintenance and not renovations and retrofits.[9] Basically, LEED for Existing Buildings: Operations & Maintenance addresses whole-building cleaning and maintenance issues (including chemical use), recycling programs, exterior maintenance programs, and systems upgrades. Nothing too difficult here.

Without focusing on existing buildings, it would be hard to reach USGBC's goal of 100,000 Green buildings across the country.

Bonus Box

Residential Real Estate Begins to Turn Green

Even though the commercial real estate industry has quickly embraced Green standards, the same isn't true of residential.

The big difference between the two markets, at least in regard to sustainability, has to do with the psychology of the deal.

First-time homeowners want to get into a new house as cheaply as possible and if going Green means an additional cost, then they would rather avoid it. Owners of existing properties are more concerned with features, like an additional room or granite countertops, that would boost value when it comes time to sell the home.

In residential, Green doesn't yet have a value proposition, but the tide is turning. Residential builders are beginning to tout Green features in their developments, although at the moment, it seems to be more of a marketing tool. However, if the industry can get over the price points issue, then the Green revolution should sweep through the residential market as it has done in commercial.

In my own state of Arizona, I had been reading about a new development called Trilogy by Shea Homes, which was launching the Shea Certified Green™, a program designed to reduce carbon footprints of homes built in its "active lifestyle" communities by 20 to 29 percent per

Continued

(Continued)

household. It seemed impressive, so I decided to call Shea Homes to see what it was all about. No one returned my telephone call. I tried again and sent an e-mail. No response.

I would like to report Trilogy is on the cutting edge of the Green movement in residential real estate, but quite frankly, I don't know. At least the company's press release was interesting: "Trilogy Homes will be built with solar technology, green fiber recycled insulation, and wood from certified sustainable forests whenever possible; they will utilize weather-responsive sprinkler systems, motion and occupancy sensor lighting, and energy efficient windows, air conditioning, appliances and more."

A number of other home builders have been sliding in the Green direction as well. KB Home began in 2008 to exclusively use Energy Star qualified refrigerators, dishwashers, and laundry appliances in its new homes. The KB Home press release was also very impressive: "KB Home has been a leader in a variety of other environmental initiatives, including protecting old growth trees in national forests from harvesting, pioneering water-wise landscaping in arid and semi-arid areas of the country, recycling demotion debris and offering zero-energy home options in select communities."

Judging by the press releases, it would seem the home builders are saving the world.

Truth be told, the Green initiatives by individual home builders have not been very aggressive or widespread. That should change when the National Association of Home Builders (NAHB) releases its National Green Building Standard, enhanced guidelines for green building practices.

The National Green Building Standard is based on the three-year-old NAHB Green Home Building Guidelines, but strengthened and expanded so it includes residential remodeling, multifamily building, and lot and site development. Like the earlier guidelines, the standard requires builders to include features in seven categories: energy, water, and resource efficiency; lot and site development; indoor environmental quality; and homeowner education.

"There are a lot of builders that have done Energy Star," says Carlos Martin, an NAHB assistant staff vice president. "What we are seeing now is that a lot of them are interested in going up a notch."

Although the NAHB boasts the mantra of "Green homes for everyone," Martin admits that going forward the industry needs to get the affordable home builders on board. "Custom builders have traditionally been at the forefront of the Green building movement," he says. "Our concern is to make sure there is an affordable version of Green home-building and there are many things that can be done that do not add a lot of cost, such as changes in materials and planning and switching fixtures and appliances."

As soon as the housing market returns to normal, expect to see more developments touting Green features, which should finally mean something to homebuyers, especially if it can be shown that the Green homes are more energy efficient and cheaper to run. It is the value proposition that will finally turn this around for the residential market.

CHAPTER SIX

MARKET FOR DISTRESSED REAL ESTATE AND LOANS

Late to develop; Keep your capital poised

During the last major real estate recession that stretched from the late 1980s through the early 1990s, Douglas Wilson, a San Diego developer, decided there was so much turmoil in the real estate markets, with builders and savings & loans failing all about him, he created an organization to help manage distressed real estate situations.

Douglas Wilson Companies, which was founded in 1989, is still around today, and busier than ever.

"I'm a bit of an early warning barometer because I get calls from lenders when things get troublesome," Wilson tells me.

"Well, when did you start getting calls?" I ask.

He replies, "About two years ago (2006)."

In retrospect, preliminary events happen in slow motion. The housing market began to stall in 2006. There were stories in the newspapers about the residential housing market being a bubble that was about to burst, but it wasn't until 2007 that problems really started to surface, finally culminating with the subprime market blowing up during the summer of that year.

Companies that invest in distressed situations began gearing up for a boom market probably as early as 2006, but definitely in the later months of 2007. The firms got funds organized, investors started depositing capital, and analysts poured over the financials of crumbling loans.

Prior to June 2007, the market was so frothy that if you had a million dollars worth of distressed loans, there would be a line out the door to buy them at 95 cents on the dollar. Today, the line is just as long, but people want to pay 40 cents on the dollar.

Where We Are Today

When I began writing this chapter in the summer of 2008, the distressed buyers were still doing the same thing—waiting. Except for occasional deals for residential loans, the market for distressed real estate hadn't yet materialized.

"We are still in a waiting period," says Wilson. "These things do lag a bit. A lot of assets the banks have on their books, problem loans, they are now trying to figure out how to liquidate these assets. Only now are we beginning to see the early stages of bulk loan sales."

Distressed buyers, many of whom were in the market during the early 1990s when billions of dollars in problem loans were unloaded to investors, expect to see similar buying opportunities in the current market collapse. However, there is a fundamental difference between the two real estate market recessions. The one in the 1980s was caused by overbuilding in the commercial sector. This time around, the imploding of real estate markets was led by residential.

Initially, the impression is, Okay, there's trouble in the housing sector; this won't affect commercial real estate. Or, commercial developers have overbuilt; this shouldn't affect residential. It just doesn't work that way, because the heart of real estate is really the financing and for the past 30 years, the same organizations have financed both sides of the market. Credit distress on one side of the real estate financing business will create liquidity problems on the other side, and vice versa.

The key point in this real estate recession and the reason for the lengthy lag between the start of the crisis and the moment distressed real estate began to hit the market in a consistent manner is that this time around it was led by residential. That is actually a messier market than commercial.

When I was discussing distressed real estate with Wilson, he told me this story: "I was on a panel recently in Las Vegas talking about distressed real estate and what everyone was saying was, one of the differences between this market crisis and the last was that with residential you have a lot more issues as compared with a dysfunctional office building in the late 1980s. Here you are dealing with homebuyers, homeowner associations, real estate regulators, and so forth. This doesn't even take into account condominiums, which are more exasperating. The residential real estate asset class has a lot more hair."

When dealing with what is called distressed real estate, in actuality, a buyer is looking at one or more of three potential situations. First, the real estate is distressed, in that it is not performing as well as the market or it needs to be rehabbed to get it to market level. A second situation is that the owner of the property is distressed and needs to sell the building rather quickly. Finally, the loan is distressed, and the lender must unload it to cleanse the balance sheets.

Even though distressed buyers and investors look for all opportunities, they focus most of their efforts on distressed loans, because if they control the loan they control the asset.

Alterra Capital Group, a distressed real estate investor in Miami, Florida, began life in a small way, buying one-off properties, either single-family residences or condo units that it could pick up inexpensively. It moved up to bulk purchases and finally around 2006, Alterra started acquiring apartment buildings.

Although Alterra was in the midst of completing some multi-family deals in Texas, Matt Wanderer, a principal with the company, tells me the distressed real estate market hadn't blossomed yet. The time was summer 2008. "It's too early," he says. "Things are just starting to trickle through."

I was a little surprised. "You're in Miami," I exclaim, "the epicenter of failed real estate; surely there must be deals."

"There are a lot of distressed sellers," he replies. "That's not good enough. In Florida, every seller is significantly distressed, but they can't give you the price you need in order to buy. Sellers cling to asset values that were in place a year before. That stalls the market."

There is a lot of deal flow, just not a lot of deals, adds David Tobin, a principal with Mission Capital Advisors in New York. "For the most part, sellers are still not willing to step up and accept the pain required to move their property—whether the seller is a major bank that's sitting on billions of dollars of busted loans or Joe Smith sitting on a second home in Boca Raton, Florida. Mr. Smith feels he's made a sacrifice by discounting his million-dollar property to $800,000, but to move it, he may have to discount it all the way down to $400,000. That's why transaction volumes have fallen off the cliff."

"What has to happen," says Wanderer, "is the banks have to admit they are distressed. The banks are going to have to acknowledge their losses. Regulatory committees are going to have to make that decision. The FDIC has to come in and say, 'Mr. Small- to Medium-Size Bank in Florida, we need you to have new appraisals on all your properties, acknowledge you are upside-down on these things and either improve reserves to hold against exposure or immediately sell.' That will trigger the buy time for distressed real estate investors in Florida."

Timing is really the issue in distressed real estate investing. Distressed investors try to gauge the bottom of the market and unfortunately as bad as things were in 2008—troubles with Fannie Mae and Freddie Mac, IndyMac, Lehman Brothers going down, and so forth—no one was thinking bottom. "It remains to be seen if we are at the bottom. I don't think we are," says Gil Tenzer, a principal in Greenwich, Connecticut-based Contrarian Capital Management LLC.

"There is still a big gap in pricing," he says, "although in many cases people are sitting on mortgages that are in excess of the property value."

Like many other distressed investors, Contrarian doesn't deal with distressed owners; it works with the lenders who are sitting on those distressed loans.

"There are billions and billions of dollars of distressed single-family residential loans, and there will be billions of dollars of distressed commercial loans," Tenzer says. "This is a problem that won't get fixed overnight. People are ignoring the fact that construction and real estate-related industries account for something like 7 to 8 percent of the U.S. GDP. An enormous reduction in activity is going to have a profound effect on the economy."

Which is, of course, why banking regulations were changed a few decades ago to force lenders to mark-to-market their loans and, in effect, encourage them to get these loans off their books so business can return to normal as quickly as possible and we all could start building and buying property once again.

In 2008, the only distressed real estate activity included a few high-profile blowups in Las Vegas and New York, land investments, and a trickle of residential loans.

"Incoming deal flow is 90 percent residential in 2008," Tobin observes. "This is where the pain is most significantly felt. What we are seeing is raw land, finished lots, condominiums, and busted condo conversion deals."

Mission Capital has been investing in finished lots. "If land plus the cost of infrastructure (roads, curb cuts, etc.) is $40,000 to $45,000 per unit, and you buy that for $20,000, you are basically not paying anything for the land," says Tobin. "Stuff is being offered at 65 to 70 cents on the dollar, but we are bidding half that."

In 2008, another distressed real estate investor picking off residential properties could be found in Westport, Connecticut. In fact, the name of the company is Westport Capital Partners LLC and it was actively buying residential mortgage loans. "We do not care about rating agency stuff or FICO scores; we understand the real estate," says Russell Bernard, managing principal of Westport Capital Partners. "We average about $200,000 a loan and we have 800 to 1,000 loans at the moment."

Bernard boasts his company buys loans one at a time, underwriting each individual loan, but Westport also acquired some pools. "We underwrote a pool in California where we expected a 30 percent default rate. So far we had no defaults; that's both good and bad news."

He adds that the nice thing about residential real estate is everybody who owns a home thinks they understand the market. "I would like to say, I drive a car, but don't put me in the Indianapolis 500. The amateur hour is over. People bought homes, flipped them, bought condos, flipped them, and it looked like easy money. But the pendulum has shifted and real estate is looking bad."

Of course, not all real estate is bad, but Bernard uses this metaphor. If you have 10 bottles of water, one is tainted and you don't know which bottle it is, then nobody drinks any of it.

Although there were some active buyers for residential in 2008, it was still a relatively sleepy year. There were really few, if any, billion-dollar portfolios of residential loans hitting the market. Part of the problem is that no one really has a handle on the ownership of those loans, as they have been pooled, securitized, sold off, then sliced and diced a couple more times. Most of us couldn't keep track of the acronyms as RMBS (residential mortgage-backed securities) morphed into CDOs (collateralized debt obligations).

"This is extremely convoluted so there has not been a lot of bulk sales," says Tobin.

In July 2008, the market finally cracked open—slightly. Merrill Lynch sold mortgage assets with an original face value of $30.6 billion that had already been written down on its books to $11.1 billion, to an affiliate of Lone Star Funds for $6.7 billion, or 22 cents for every dollar of face value.[1]

Also stranded without buyers are owners of condominiums and busted condo projects. Individual condo units, which are generally not the targets of distressed real estate buyers and condominium projects, especially in places like Florida, were much too uncertain as of 2008. Certainly the bottom had not been hit yet.

As for condo projects, the complexity has been mind-boggling.

"No one has figured out the busted condo yet," says Alterra's Wanderer.

It will take someone willing to go through a trial and error process, hoping to figure out how to handle bulk holdings within a homeowner's association. There are all kinds of complications in terms of short falls to the association. Suppose you have 200 apartments and 100 were sold as condos. The owners want to sell the other 100 in bulk, but half of the sold units are going through various stages of foreclosure and the owners have decided not to pay their fees. Do you let the homeowner's association go into default, in which case it can't pay insurance and electric bills and the whole deal goes wrong?

Opportunities in Commercial Real Estate

As noted, the last major real estate recession that ended in the early 1990s was partly caused by overbuilding in the commercial sector. Developers and lenders seemed to have learned their lesson from that disaster and in the 20 years since, supply has been fairly restrained.

One result of forbearance in the commercial real estate market has been relatively decent fundamentals with occupancy and rents going in the right direction.

"From 2004 to 2007, we had reasonably good property fundamentals," avers Ray Milnes, National Industry Sector Leader for real estate at KPMG. "The overall U.S. economy was doing okay. There was a limited amount of new supply on the market so consequently commercial real estate owners experienced real rental increases."

That period of complacency began to dissolve in 2007 with the onset of the credit crisis and the slowing of the economy. Building tenants began to get more conservative on space requirements and demand softened.

As we have seen in previous chapters, the problem with commercial real estate, whether it was high-rise office buildings, suburban office parks, shopping centers, or multifamily development is that there was so much cheap capital available, investors couldn't stop buying this stuff. Prices skyrocketed and cap rates declined. For some products, cap rates dropped below 5 percent, which meant the investment was yielding slightly more than a bond and real estate had so much more risk.

The façade of commercial real estate stability was weak in other regards as well. Buyers supported the ever-increasing price of their investments with dubious cash flow expectations. In other words, future rent growth would support higher valuations. This worked for a while, at least until mid-year 2007. After that, rents began heading in the opposite direction as vacancies started to rise.

Second, since there was a lot of cheap capital available for acquisitions, investors would leverage to the hilt, adding short-term and mezzanine debt into the deal, so the amount of equity needed was minimal, as low as 5 percent. Buyers assumed it would be easy to refinance that expensive mezzanine debt. As guys like Harry Macklowe found out, that is no longer the case. At some point in the near future, a lot of short-term loans are going to be coming due and that could force more commercial real estate into the market.

Third, lenders were able to offer cheap capital for acquisitions because they were repackaging, securitizing, and selling the debt as commercial mortgage-backed securities and collateralized debt obligations.

"Lenders would originate loans, sell them into these CMBS and CDO vehicles and other investors would buy this paper," Milnes explains. "The financiers made a lot of money off the fees involved in securitization, so they continued to originate more loans, sell more CMBS, and generate more fees. Meanwhile, they lost their way as to sound, fundamental loan underwriting."

In short, a lot of these loans shouldn't have been made—and they especially shouldn't have been made with high leverage.

Despite all that, very little commercial real estate or commercial real estate loans have come into the market in distressed condition. In fact, Milnes says, at mid-year 2008, the percentage of commercial real estate foreclosures was extremely low, about 3 percent of total loans outstanding.

Except for multifamily, where new leases are essentially written every year, most commercial is done with long leases, at least 7 to 10 years, so if there are industrywide problems they don't tend to show up immediately. The first properties to return to the market because of distressed financials will be those acquired late in the 2005–2007 cycle, highly leveraged and with short-term debt. A few of these properties already came back to market in 2008, but I expect to see much more before the end of the decade.

"From 2005 to 2007, the old loan underwriting rules were thrown out," suggests Richard Berry, a principal in Robert Sheridan & Partners LLC in River Forest, Illinois. "On a transaction, it used to be that 75 to 80 percent of the deal involved debt and the rest was equity. During the years I just mentioned, you could get an 80 percent loan plus mezzanine debt and that could easily take you to 95 percent debt and only 5 percent equity. Values have since come down and these properties are probably underwater."

The real distressed activity, however, won't occur until the banks confess to their losses and that won't happen until the regulators force them to do so. "These are loans that may not have been foreclosed," says Milnes, "but the regulatory requirements don't allow you to wait until there is an official bad act. Rather, the regulators make the banks mark these loans to market on their books."

If one just looks at the highly leveraged lending, then all commercial real estate seems to be trending in the same direction in regard to potential distressed situations; operationally though, they behave differently. Due to the long-term leases in the office sector, Mission Capital's Tobin doesn't expect to see a lot of this type of product hit the market anytime soon. On the other hand, the hotel market is getting choppy, and Tobin predicts that a surprising amount of lodging debt could be had cheaply come 2009. And Tobin is not at all sanguine about retail, which he calls "dicey."

"I looked at some Goldman Sachs' research," says Tobin, "and it estimates that total defaults in commercial will be roughly on par with subprime mortgage-related loans. That's about $200 billion in bad loans."

In 2008, barely any of these commercial bad loans had come to market. "The banks are hiding their heads (and their loans?) in the sand," Tobin says. His prediction: Many of the distressed commercial loans will surface in 2009 and 2010.

Where We Are Headed

Many smaller community banks were shut out of the commercial real estate loan market because they couldn't compete with the conduits, which eventually securitized their loans into CMBS and CDOs. That, as it turned out, was good news. Unfortunately, these same banks seeking different markets instead lent capital for condominium projects, condo-conversions, land loans, and builder loans—individually or collectively the most distressed of all real estate sectors.

"If you look at some of these banks, over half of their loans are in the commercial real estate mortgage area (condos, land, and builder loans) and a significant portion of these are bad," says Berry. "The write-offs will be far greater than the remaining capital."

What Berry expects is a wave of bank failures.

"When a bank has residential on its balance sheets, these are single-family loans, but condo-conversion loans, new condo development loans, and land loans to home builders—these are commercial real estate loans," he explains. "At mid-year 2008, they were still being carried as 'current.'"

Starting in 2006, Berry's firm, Robert Sheridan & Partners, raised considerable capital from institutional investors to acquire distressed real estate and loans. So far it has not invested any of the money in its fund.

"Toward the end of 2007, we thought the time was near," says Berry. "Then by 2008, we thought the banks would be writing down these loans. It has not happened. The banks are not doing this voluntarily because once they do, some of these banks will be simultaneously shutting their doors."

As an example, Berry says in early 2008 he scrutinized the books of a small community bank and it had 80 percent of its loans in commercial real estate (condos, land loans, etc.).

Getting the banks to admit that they have made bad loans will be up to the regulators, and Berry doesn't see this happening until 2009. "It's just a matter of time, and when it does happen it won't be pretty."

The week that I was working on this chapter, the markets were roiled by a shareholder run on Fannie Mae and Freddie Mac and the federal government's seizure of IndyMac Bank.

As the *Wall Street Journal* reported, "Although roughly a year has passed since credit conditions began to tighten, wreaking havoc on capital markets, many traditional banks are just now starting to feel the effects of a rising number of borrowers who can't pay back loans. Adding to the problem is that banks that need to shore up their balance sheets are beginning to have trouble attracting capital from investors."[2]

"We will see a lot more struggling, if not failing, banks," observes Spencer Garfield, managing director of Hudson Realty Capital. "A lot of loans will be sold at discounts, a lot of institutions will be taking significant write-downs, and many lenders are in jeopardy of going out of business."

In September 2008, Washington Mutual Inc. was on the verge of collapse and ended up being acquired by JPMorgan Chase & Co. It remains to be seen how JPMorgan will handle the thrift's portfolio of troubled mortgage loans.

If the last real estate recession, when a tremendous number of thrifts failed and were taken over by the federal government, is any model for what will happen this time around, then one should expect a lengthy, two-stage market for distressed loans.

The last time the country went through a similar episode, financial and real estate industries wallowed in a deep trough for about three years, from about 1989 through 1991, as the regulators, investors, and everyone else involved tried to sort out the damage done to the various real estate markets. Once the regulators and markets were able to get a handle on the crisis, then a massive deleveraging and reinvestment took place, and it did so in a fairly orderly manner. Although financial historians may debate the exact timetable, over a three-year period, from around 1992 to 1994, most of the problem real estate and broken loans were in the hands of new investors. In effect, the window for distressed investing did not last very long.

All real estate markets behave differently all the time. Geographically, one city will prosper while another falls into recession; sectorwise, single-family residential markets may weaken but multifamily may strengthen. For argument's sake, if I were to choose a general starting point when most real estate markets began to falter in this downturn, I would pick mid-year 2006 and not 2007 when the first crisis—subprime mortgages—erupted. If I'm close to accurate, then the trough in this recession should stretch to around mid-year 2009. If you're one of those people who feels 2007 should be the starting point, then the trough will go into 2010.

In either case, early distressed real estate investors—and many in 2008 were poised to strike, but didn't—will be active in 2009 and 2010. Deal flow should hit peak in 2011 and 2012. After that comes recovery.

Sounding out a number of distressed real estate investors, this is the consensus of opinion.

"The distressed debt market is upon us (summer 2008)," says Garfield, "and it will really rear its head in the next 12 months and then there will be a prevalent debt market that will run into 2010 or 2011. About that time, capital will be coming back into the market. By 2014 or 2015, we'll be back to another strong lending environment."

Here's a similar view. "It's going to take about three years to clear out the muck," says Wilson. "It will be a painful three-year cycle, but at that point banks will need to get their one asset— capital—out working again."

"The real volume of distressed real estate transactions will be from 2010 to 2012," says Berry.

Wilson optimistically notes, "We will look back on this five years (2012) from now and say, 'We survived another one.'"

"Given the way the economy is going at mid-year 2008 (adding fuel to a smoldering real estate recession), expect more bad incidents and adjustments to come along," says Milnes. "In 2009, institutions and some property owners that just can't stand the heat anymore are going to get rid of this stuff. We're in for some troubled times as it relates to the owners of properties that were highly leveraged. Financial institutions are going to have to move things by 2009. There will be good opportunities for buyers of distressed real estate (and loans!) from 2009 through 2011."

Milnes cautions, "The window is never open for very long."

Bonus Box

Hospitality Industry Is Not Distressed

In 2008, hospitality industry diviners were particularly active, trying to interpret the myriad portents that suddenly came tumbling one upon the other in its direction: high energy costs, overstuffed pipeline, softening economy, and sinking revenue per available room, or in industry lingo, Revpar.

If it all looked like a cauldron full of bad news, well, it was. But as Madonna almost sung, "Don't Cry for Me, Travel Argentina."

The always cyclical hospitality industry has ridden dramatic roller coaster curves for the past 20 years and as it swooshes through the current economic downturn, the diviners take great pains to point out this industry is coming off a great high and the subsequent trough will be moderate in depth and length. Consider hospitality a nondistressed asset for the moment.

"You have to remember that 2007 was a record-setting year in profitability throughout the industry," says Patrick Ford, president of Lodging Econometrics. "The hotel business is softening, but it is not depressed."

Despite the optimism, the hospitality industry does face some tough situations. First, industry performance is weakening just as a ton of new supply is about to enter the market.

In July 2008, just a day before Marriott International would report its earnings (very weak!), the financial press noted, "Its stock price has been cut in half since peaking in April 2007. A big problem for Marriott and other hoteliers is that the supply of available rooms has been growing while demand has slipped, an age-old problem for the cyclical industry."[3]

At the end of the first quarter 2008, Lodging Econometrics reported a record pipeline of 5,807 projects with 779,307 guest rooms. Four months later, Lodging Econometrics' Ford was busy calculating the numbers for his next report. "I can tell you that developers' sentiment has changed considerably and the lending crisis has caught up with hotel development," he says. "The market is radically different today than it was at the end of the first quarter." As it turned out, by the second quarter, the lodging market hit a new peak: 5,883 projects in the pipeline with 785,547 guest rooms. "The market appears to be cresting," Ford notes.

That record pipeline started to diverge into three approaches: those developers with financing and a project on the ground will open hotels in 2008 and 2009; those developers who announced a project and didn't yet get financing will delay the project; or those developers who announced a project and didn't yet get financing will cancel the project.

In a bit of horror to the industry, there were a lot of projects financed already and many will come online in 2008 and 2009, making a tough market worse. Is it an excess of supply? Ford parses his words carefully, "It may look like a supply problem, but it is actually a disappearance of demand problem."

The second major problem is the high cost of fuel.

As I have mentioned often, I live in Mesa, Arizona, very near Scottsdale and Phoenix. During the summer of 2008, the Arizona newspapers were full of stories about the local lodging market weakening as gasoline prices passed $4 a gallon. As it turned out, high prices at the pump was not a great concern.

"High gasoline costs will affect the low end of the market," says Jack Corgel, who holds the Robert C. Baker Chair of Real Estate at Cornell University's School of Hotel Administration. "Certainly, limited service markets will feel the pinch from moderate income families cutting back on road trips. Most people who have substantial incomes probably won't cut back on their travel."

The real problem, Corgel notes, is how the high price of fuel is affecting the airlines—and that could have a major impact on the hospitality industry.

The airline industry and the lodging market grasp tightly in a symbiotic relationship. So, with the airline companies contending with high jet fuel costs, which has caused profitability to disappear and balance sheets to bleed red, one solution has been to reduce capacity, and that's a problem for the lodging industry.

"Under a worst-case scenario, a 1 percent decline in the number of seats flown within the United States will result in a 0.39 percent decline in demand at the nation's hotels," reports Mark Woodworth, president of PKF Hospitality Research. "If airline capacity is reduced by 10 percent as some have suggested, then lodging demand would fall 3.9 percent. To put this in perspective, the decline in lodging demand experienced in 2001 was just 3.3 percent." (In 2001 the terrorist attacks on the World Trade Center and the Pentagon were the beginning of a serious hotel industry recession.)

"If the worst-case scenario in regard to the airline industry plays out, the effects on the lodging industry would be varied," suggests

Continued

(Continued)

Kapila Anand, hospitality industry sector leader for KPMG International. "Certain brands will be hit, others less so. The business traveler who would normally stay at the high end of the marketplace will trade down. We are already seeing this."

Other problems will occur in the secondary markets. "The hospitality business in secondary communities is more reliant on road and airline access," says Anand. "If you are in a secondary or tertiary market with a high-end hotel, unless there is some other attraction nearby, you should be concerned."

If one charted the hotel industry since the 1980s, the roller coaster graph would start with a deep slope downward during the great real estate downturn of the late 1980s and 1990s, then from around 1994 through 2001, a gradual ascent built on good fortune. By the time 2001 rolled around, the tech bubble had burst causing a minor recession, the terrorists had done their damage scaring most people out of traveling, and all this was followed by the SARS crisis, which frightened everyone else from traveling.

After a couple of grim years, it all came together for the lodging industry and by mid-2003 good tidings began to roll: occupancies rose, rates improved, Revpar soared. All data points were heading in the right direction and remained that way until 2007, when demand began to ease—although room rates were still heading north.

Demand eased for a short period of time in 2007, says Woodworth, then actually took off again through the remainder of the year. By early 2008, demand softened once again, this time to a weakening economy. "We had this double dip phenomenon that we had never seen before in the domestic lodging industry," says Woodworth, "and we are concerned because while we have demand, declining average room rates are being hurt. In addition, so many developers were able to get their deals done that the level of new supply opening in 2008 and 2009 is going to be above the long-run average."

In essence, for the remainder of this decade, demand will be contracting while supply expands.

No cause to panic, says Cornell's Corgel, as average daily room rates are simply moderating from a 4 to 6 percent growth rate down to 2 to 3 percent and Revpar growth will drop down into the 1.5 percent range. Sure, it's not as good as the 6 to 7 percent growth rate earlier in the decade, but it's not negative growth, either.

A lot of projects came online in 2007 and 2008 and that will impact the market through 2009, notes Ted Mandigo, a principal and director of TR Mandigo & Co., a Chicago-based hospitality consulting firm. "Projects beyond that are in the early stages of getting canceled or put on the back burner. Future pipeline growth will diminish and that will give us a breather to absorb this current peak of construction."

Mandigo expects average occupancy rates will drop 2 to 3 percent by 2009. In the Chicago market, where he is located, Mandigo, for example, predicts the occupancy rate for area hotels will stay above 70 percent. The decline will be sharper elsewhere such as on the East Coast, but it will be coming off a strong 80 percent occupancy level.

Mandigo, as well as other lodging industry consultants, doesn't believe the current softness in industry performance will be overwhelming and the industry will stabilize as early as 2010, with a firm uptick starting in 2011.

The level of confidence is so strong, PKF's Woodworth is suggesting to investors that this actually is a good time to buy hotel properties. On the other hand, he is also telling his clients not to sell.

"Earnings are going to be down, below average this year and even the next," he elucidates. "Interest rates are going up, causing cap rates to escalate. The combination of declining incomes and escalating cap rates will lead to lower value. I'm telling my clients, if you don't have to sell, then hold out and let the markets recover. Similarly, I'm also recommending they not refinance if they don't have to, mainly because debt is hard to get and very expensive when you do get it."

The one cautionary note comes from Cornell's Corgel. "The lodging industry moves with the economy and if the country avoids a deep recession and energy prices drop back a bit," he says, "then we will have a good lodging market in 2010. If both those things do not happen, then the lodging market will be hanging by its fingernails just to stay even."

PART III

RESIDENTIAL REAL ESTATE

CHAPTER SEVEN

THE SINGLE-FAMILY HOUSING MARKET

We've all been beaten up pretty well by now;
Better times come with a new decade

Thursday, July 24, 2008, was somewhat of a hallmark day for me in regard to this book. I had saved the chapter on single-family housing for last, mostly because the residential real estate story was still evolving, and I wanted the chapter to be as fresh as I could make it before bundling off the manuscript to the publisher.

On that Thursday, I did two lengthy interviews for the chapter, one of which was a morning discussion with Jed Smith, the managing director of quantitative research for the National Association of Realtors, who surprised me with a persistently upbeat analysis of the housing market. His basic message was we had hit bottom and by 2009 the single-family housing market would show a vital upswing in sales.

Later that afternoon I picked up the *Wall Street Journal*, which ran an interesting column off the front page of the "Money & Investing" section. The *Journal* reported the homeowner vacancy rate, or the percentage of available housing stock sitting empty and waiting to be sold (not occupied homes where a seller can be a patient seller), rose to a record 2.9 percent in the first quarter 2008 compared with a long-term average of roughly 1.5 percent. This rate didn't include foreclosed homes tied up in legal proceedings or empty houses that had been pulled from a slumping market. The key point of the column was this: To get the vacancy rate back to something like normal, about 1 million homes would have to find new owners.[1]

With just five months left in 2008, that seemed like an impossibility.

But, what else happened that Thursday? Well, the stock market folded almost 300 points, mostly because of the bad news coming from the nation's housing market. Coincidentally, the National Association of Realtors (yes, Jed Smith's organization) reported existing home sales dropped 2.6 percent to a seasonally adjusted annual rate of 4.86 million units in June, a 15.5 percent decline from the same period the year before. In addition, the median home price swooned 6.1 percent from the previous year. Both numbers were deeper than analysts expected.[2]

The NAR blamed the price decline on the amount of foreclosed properties coming back into the market. That situation in July wasn't getting any better. The very next day, the financial press reported the number of households facing the foreclosure process more than doubled in the second quarter 2008 as compared to the year before. When the final numbers are tallied for 2008, an estimated 2.5 million homes will have entered the foreclosure process, up from 1.5 million the year before.[3]

This isn't to say that Jed Smith is wrong. Perhaps 2008 is the bottom of the market. Unfortunately, when real estate bubbles burst, markets can stay in or near the bottom for a number of years.

As real estate recession downturns go, this one at the end of the first decade of this century is a little different because it is a wee bit more complicated. "We have gone quite a ways past just the normal type of weak housing market," notes Jonathan Dienhart, director of published research with Hanley Wood Market Intelligence. "There are broader issues this time around, problems with mortgage finance and the banking industry. Overall, I don't think we have seen all the chips fall."

Some economists and business publications were reporting a housing bubble as early as 2005, but forward momentum by home builders, speculators, banks, investors, Wall Street, indeed all the players in the industry, was so strong the great deflation didn't happen until 2007. One might say the pinprick, or the great deflator, didn't come from the housing industry per se but from the mortgage side of the business.

Where We Were

There are probably 50 reasons why the country fell into a profound real estate downturn and credit crisis, but if we isolate just a small group of interrelated factors, we can more easily understand what happened to the country's residential real estate markets.

After the tech bubble burst at the end of the last decade and then the terrorist strikes in 2001, the country entered into a mild recession. Meanwhile, the housing industry, which had been strongly pummeled in the late 1980s, began a decade-long upswing. From a cyclical standpoint, the single-family housing market probably would have started to swoon at the start of this decade, but the Federal Reserve decided to help the economy out of the recession by keeping interest rates low. This had the two-pronged ancillary effect of prolonging the upswing in the housing cycle and pumping up single-family residential market performance with steroid-like enhancements much above and beyond normality.

The housing market was able to keep going strong because of what was happening on Wall Street. Investment banks had been buying mortgages, packaging them into large pools, slicing and dicing the pools into traunches based on risk, and selling them as investment vehicles called mortgage-backed securities. By this new decade, Wall Street had refined and overengineered the process so they could, in fact, sell securities reformulated from other securities. This was all great for Wall Street because every time they sold a mortgage-backed security, the investment banks booked gobs of fees.

Obviously, there had to be a market for mortgage-backed securities. And there was—everywhere around the world. Unlike in the United States, where people spend all they earn, in many developing countries, such as China, citizens save. Cumulatively this saved money doesn't have an investment outlet big enough in the homeland, so the financial infrastructure of countries in Europe and Asia invests elsewhere around the world, such as in mortgage-backed securities designed and constructed in the United States.

So, let's work backward along this chain. Global investors need investments, so they turn to Wall Street; Wall Street creates mortgage-based investments; it turns to mortgage originators for more product. Mortgage originators create more types of mortgages; they turn to home builders to build more homes so they can sell more mortgages. Home builders construct more and more residences.

The end of this daisy chain came in two phases. The first was slow and easy, the second was a free fall.

"The precipitating factor was affordability," explains Richard DeKaser, chief economist at National City Corporation. "If you look at the basic affordability calculation, how much a typical family's money is required in order to buy the typical home, 1998 was the best year and things didn't get any worse until early in the decade because the Federal Reserve was cutting interest rates. But, by 2005, interest rates were no longer falling and that, combined with rising home prices, increased the pain on homebuyers to the point where demand began to back off."

At this juncture, the housing market made a smooth cyclical adjustment: demand diminished, sales declined, and price appreciation began to fade.

The trouble was that many of the innovative loan products created to induce more people to get more mortgages and to buy more homes only made sense when home prices were climbing. When price appreciation stopped, these loans were suddenly very risky.

Eventually institutional investors worldwide caught on. There was, despite what the rating agencies were saying, an outsized risk in these mortgage-backed investments and they stopped buying— literally overnight. That's when the whole finance/mortgage/real estate market fell apart.

"I was surprised at how quickly this all unraveled," says DeKaser. "As recently as March 2007, you were seeing subprime mortgages being packaged and sold to the secondary market, including foreign investors, at a very healthy pace. In the first quarter 2007, subprime accounted for 50 percent of all mortgage-backed securities issuances. That was as high as it had ever been. By August, there were almost no buyers. Since the fourth quarter 2007, subprime mortgage-backed issuance has been zero."

In effect, DeKaser adds, the change represented the recognition "that the things everyone thought were the greatest invention since sliced bread were suddenly perceived to be toxic. The investment community abandoned the market overnight."

Quality was definitely a problem with many of the mortgages pumped out mid-decade. Think of it this way: If I'm the guy who is making the loan at the local bank and I can turn the loan around and sell it to you and you are going to package it up and securitize it, I don't have the same incentive to make sure the person I am giving the loan to is a quality borrower because I am not the one who is going to bear the brunt of the pain if the borrower defaults.

This was phase two of the housing market correction, and we are still in the middle of it. In 2008, the problems that began with some of the subprime mortgages spread to the prime mortgage side of the business. A major concern for banks in 2008 was that housing prices declined as foreclosures mounted, so no one could get an estimate of the write-offs the banks would actually have to take.[4]

Where We Are Today

It's important to reiterate that housing markets do not all move in the same manner nor at the same time, so even in the current downturn, some major metropolitan areas in North Carolina and Texas have managed to remain stable, while everywhere else troubles gather.

"Downturns in the early 1980s and 1990s were not as sharp or as synchronized across the country as in the downturn today," observes Matthew Anderson, a principal in Foresight Analytics LLC, a provider of real estate market data. "In those past downturns, you had 50 to 60 percent of the markets in decline at any point in time. In the first quarter 2008, prices were falling in 75 percent of the metro areas around the country. That is unprecedented."

In May 2008, the Standard & Poor's/Case-Schiller 20-City Index showed home values had fallen 18.4 percent since peak in July 2006.[5]

"The Case-Schiller index is approaching a 20 percent decline. Expect another 10 percent, maybe as much as 15 percent, decline in housing prices," says Peter Hooper, managing director and chief economist at Deutsche Bank Securities. "We are a little over halfway down in terms of house price declines."

Celia Chen, the director of housing economics at Moody's Economy.com concurs. "Home prices will eventually fall 20 to

25 percent," she says. "If it hits 25 percent, it would be the worst downturn since World War II."

Although those numbers sound dire, don't forget the market is coming off a record time when home prices in some cities doubled. In that context, a 25 percent adjustment doesn't seem too bad.

"Between 1996 and 2006, real home prices rose by 52 percent and far outpaced gains in per capita personal income," says Jared Sullivan, an economist with CBRE/Torto Wheaton Research. "Such large gains were simply not sustainable. In fact, growth in house prices during the residential real estate bubble surpassed per income growth by a staggering 41 percent. It was all fueled by low interest rates, creative mortgage products, and lax lending standards."

Weighing on home price direction are two opposing forces. First, the number of houses under construction has fallen dramatically. That will be helpful. The number of housing starts, which had been climbing from a fairly high number, reached 1.6 million starts in 2000, and then jumped to a frothy 2.1 million starts in 2005, reports the National Association of Realtors. The housing start numbers for 2008 will probably end up in the 1 million starts range and could dip even lower in 2009.

"From a supply and demand perspective, if the supply continues to grow at massive rates and the demand does not change, prices are going to continue to fall," explains Sullivan. "We need to see a contraction in the supply. In 2007 and 2008 the market slowed but not nearly to the levels we needed to get to."

At the other end of the scale, home prices are being undercut by the increasing amount of foreclosures coming into the market. If 2008 looked bad, 2009 may not be an improvement.

"Generally speaking, banks have been holding back on aggressive sales tactics, like cutting prices dramatically in order to move bad loans off the balance sheet," says Anderson. "By mid-year 2008, they hadn't capitulated yet, having decided there is no near-term improvement in sight. But financial institutions have been under so much stress for so long, they are getting tired and want to get rid of all those bad loans."

Anderson was hoping the banks would start moving bad loans by fourth quarter 2008 to allow for the beginnings of market stabilization in 2009.

The typical mortgage loan will go delinquent after 30 or 60 days of nonpayment, but these days there is a huge variance as banks are trying to keep homeowners in their houses, so delinquencies may not happen for six months. The same kind of stretching out has been happening in foreclosures, says Glenn Schultz, a managing director and head of asset-backed securities and nonagency mortgage research at Wachovia Securities. "The average foreclosure time for a subprime mortgage is 12 months, but the line is being pushed out to 24 months. It's like watching a pig move through a pipeline."

Schultz doesn't expect the big wave of foreclosures to clear out of the market until mid-year 2009.

In April 2008, mortgage holders and investors found they now owned 660,000 foreclosed homes, up from 493,000 in January 2008. The surge in foreclosures meant the inventory of bank-owned homes, known as REO (real estate owned) increased, leading Mark Zandi, chief economist at Moody's Economy.com, to predict the inventory of REO homes won't peak before the end of 2009.[6]

In July 2008, about 721,000 foreclosed homes were on the market nationwide. That was up from 112,000 in July 2007, reported analysts from Barclays Capital, who also predicted the total to rise 60 percent before peaking in late 2009.[7]

About the only good news in 2008 was that the decline in home sales slowed. Even that, however, was not totally positive because most of the market was being flooded by foreclosures. "About one-fourth of all sales in the United States (summer 2008) were either foreclosures or short-sales (sold for less than owed on mortgage)," says Chen.

By mid-year 2008, single-family home sales dropped 36 percent, the second worst experience since the Great Depression of the 1930s. (From 1979 to 1982—a period of double-digit inflation— home sales fell 52 percent.) Again, the positive spin is that the decline in home sales was bottoming out. "If you were to create a chart of new and existing home sales, you would see an absolutely precipitous decline over the course of 2007," says DeKaser. "That decline has almost plateaued. Maybe it will continue to move down a little bit, but the worst declines have greatly diminished. Sales are now in the process of bottoming."

The proper perspective on home sales is that 10 years ago, U.S. real estate agents sold 5 million homes annually, says Smith, but then in 2004 they sold a record 7.5 million homes. That was followed by 7 million homes in 2005, 6.5 million in 2006, 5.65 million in 2007, and an estimated 5.39 million in 2008. "Now everybody asks, 'When are we going to have that recovery?'" says NAR's Smith, but 5 million home sales annually was a pretty good tally a few years ago. We just got used to higher numbers."

Where We Are Headed

"Here's an interesting point," says Smith. "The country is now selling homes at the pace of 10 years ago, but over that period of time, the country's population has grown, the number of people in households has increased, and incomes are up. In other words, there is a pent-up demand for homes."

Smith is one of the few economists and researchers who is predicting a fast turnaround out of the housing slump. He says existing home sales will start climbing again in 2009 to 5.71 million units sold; new home sales will hit bottom in 2008 at 0.54 million, and then will push forward in 2009 to 0.59 million; and even housing starts will be up: 0.97 million in 2009.

Smith is a demographics kind of guy and this is what he sees: Every year 1.3 million to 1.5 million new households are formed. Also, every year about 300,000 homes are demolished, so just to stay even the country needs to build 1.6 to 1.8 million new homes to keep up with the population and replace demolition. Hence, demographics will save the housing market.

National City's DeKaser is in the Smith camp. "We do have a fundamental need for housing," he says. "Our population continues to grow and housing is relatively cheap now. The declines we have experienced have pushed pricing back to the affordable level rather than the unaffordable situation we had three years ago. So, housing affordability has improved. The only thing holding back housing is the weakness in the mortgage market, the deep pessimism by investors, and tremendous uncertainties around the other questions such as how far prices will fall."

One outlook on the mortgage market comes from Hanley Wood's Dienhart, who notes, "I don't think the mortgage market will get significantly worse, but things continue to drop all the time with the various financial institutions. By 2010, the mortgage market should be stabilized. It still won't be easy to get a loan, but future mortgages that are given will be better from a risk assessment standpoint."

"The private mortgage market in 2008 was dead," says Chen. "Before demand can be strong for housing, before households can get credit the same way they did before the market excesses occurred, the private market has to come back and develop new products. I don't know how the mortgage industry is going to re-create itself, but it has to do that before liquidity is added so the housing market can get back to a normal state."

Smith and DeKaser make a good point about demographics and population growth for the long term. Next year is just too soon for a housing market turnaround. Stabilization, bottom of the trough, and so forth, could happen sometime in 2009, but a rebound in prices? The optimists suggest the next decade at the earliest.

Housing is the future, but getting from here to there won't be easy. Perhaps the most conservative estimate of market recovery comes from Dienhart, who also believes in the zen of demographics.

"The long-term picture for housing has to be one of expansion, because we see it in the demographics. More people will want to live in more places," says Dienhart. "Unfortunately, what we are looking at in the short term is 12 to 24 months of substantial troubles. The country faces a lot of challenges due to how widespread the credit crisis has become. It will be 10 years (2018) before the housing industry gets back on the track of expansion."

"Home prices should stop falling by 2009," opines Foresight Analytics' Anderson, "and from then on a few markets may see some incremental increases in home prices. It just won't be many. Maybe by 2012 there will be a little more home price appreciation."

"The country could see a gradual pickup in home sales as we go through 2009 into 2010," adds Deutsche Bank's Hooper, "but no meaningful pickup in home prices until after that. The markets won't get back to normalcy at least until 2011. We have to see where the economy is going. My sense is that housing was the engine of growth for quite awhile and with consumers taking a big hit on the asset side of the balance sheet, they may feel a need to be saving more. We have to get past this decade before we see a significant rebound in the housing market."

When a bubble market bursts, left behind is a lot of carnage and it takes about three years for markets just to get a handle on the mess. By all measures, the housing boom was over in 2006 and the mortgage market fell apart around mid-year 2007. At mid-year 2008, smaller banks were failing, Fannie Mae and Freddie Mac suffered a few market scares, and the investment banks such as Merrill Lynch were still trying to raise capital. A lot of potholes surfaced in 2008.

"It will take quite a bit of time to clear out the problems that have occurred in the mortgage market. They are significant," avers Chen. "There was a lot of excess that occurred during the housing boom in terms of lending and new products that were not well thought out. That's part of the reason we don't expect significant activity until 2010."

The next housing cycle will take place between 2011 and 2015, Chen suggests. Just don't expect to see the same kind of price growth that occurred in the first decade of the new century. At best, home prices from 2011 through 2015 will rise about 1 to 1.5 percent greater than inflation.

New families entering the housing market and investors circling the carcasses of the housing industry looking for deals in 2008 through 2009 will be able to take advantage of the current market weakness, but only time will tell if those investments will pay off in a meaningful way. By consensus opinion, anything bought today probably won't look like a good investment until around 2013.

"I would be very surprised if the country experienced another housing boom in the next decade in terms of new construction and home pricing," says Anderson. "If we do have another bubble, it will be in a different sector, other than housing. The idea of guaranteed price increase in housing is not a firm belief the next generation is going to hold to."

Bonus Box

Seniors Housing Is Not Distressed

The seniors housing industry parallels the hospitality industry in a couple of odd ways. The most apparent for the purposes of this book is to say right off, seniors housing is also not a distressed real estate sector.

Seniors housing has maintained stable operating and investment environments at the end of the first decade of this century because, like the hospitality industry, it went through some tough times at the turn of the century, quickly righted itself, and starting about 2004 experienced record years in terms of occupancy, rate growth, and net operating income. The current economic downturn and credit crisis has certainly diminished the market, but again, like hospitality, declines have come off record-setting years.

From about 2003 to 2008, the seniors housing industry had "a very strong run," notes Robert Kramer, president of the National Investment Center for the Seniors Housing & Care Industry, known mostly by its acronym, NIC. "About mid-year 2007, the industry reached record highs across all the different care segments; median occupancies were in the 94 to 97 percent range and average occupancies in the 91 to 93 percent range with rates increasing between 5 to 7 percent a year."

In the first quarter 2008, average occupancy rates stood at 92.1 percent, a slight decline from the same period the year before, NIC reports.[8]

A second important way seniors housing is similar to the hospitality industry is that it is an operating-intensive business that works off a real estate platform. However, here is where the two industries differ. In the more mature hospitality industry, real estate has for the most part separated from the operating companies. So, for example, one company might own 100 Marriott properties, but that ownership entity is not a part of the hospitality giant Marriott International Inc. That kind of overall sector separation has not been attained yet in seniors housing.

Seniors housing in the forms we know today—senior apartments, independent living, assisted living, and dementia and nursing care—erupted as an asset class in the 1980s and has gone through some very painful growing cycles in its short history.

The first spurt of building was aimed for the aging World War II generation. Unfortunately, its aim was off because the first generation of seniors housing was marketed to folks from 65 to 75 years of age, only to learn that people who moved into seniors housing were in their eighties; a boom/bust period. Then in the 1990s, the assisted living concept was pioneered and enthusiasm for this product engendered another building boom, which was followed by another bust.

"The short version of what happened was aggressive capital chased a recently introduced product type called assisted living, which new owners were pretty much learning how to operate as they went along," says Mel Gamzon, president of Seniors Housing Investment Advisors. "Between the bullshit, the developers and operators, and financing sources, things got out of sorts."

A look at construction data for seniors housing as tallied by the American Seniors Housing Association (ASHA) shows that almost

Continued

(Continued)

66,000 units came online in 1999. Then the market deflated with 35,305 new units in 2000, 28,964 new units in 2001, and a recent low water mark of 21,495 in 2002. By the next year, seniors housing stabilized, and the market had slowly been climbing back until the economic slowdown and credit crunch engulfed the country starting in 2007.

"We have had a lot less development over the last six years, which put us well below demographic growth," observes Raymond Lewis, CIO and executive vice president of Ventas Inc., a Louisville, Kentucky-based seniors housing company. "In 2008, there probably won't be more than 17,000 units built, half of that being assisted living, but there will be much more than 17,000 people turning 85 in 2008."

According to a report by ASHA, about 18 million people were in the 75+ age bracket in 2005, and those numbers will slowly rise through the next decade. By 2020, the leading edge of the baby boomers will start hitting the age of 75, and then growth in this age bracket will blossom very quickly.

The economic slowdown and credit crisis, stringent underwriting guidelines, and a tough market for entitlements are all conspiring to constrict new development in seniors housing. Yet, as Gamzon points out, "We have a tsunami of demographics moving in the right direction. And if we look at the supply that is not being added, that is really a helluva megatrend."

In regard to future prospects, there are two ways to look at seniors housing. The first is demographics, and this is really a story of destiny forestalled because the leading edge of the baby boomers won't wash into this sector in a big way for another 15 years.

The second viewpoint is market penetration.

"Demographics are not driving the growth of this industry," maintains Kramer. "What is driving the industry is absorption and demand. As new supply comes on the market, it is being absorbed. Why? Because a greater percentage of the targeted age group likes and accepts this product."

Kramer likes to cite a national housing study of adults aged 75 and older. When they were asked the question "Do you look at independent living for you personally as an option?," 13 percent answered that it was a "very desirable option." Yet, says Kramer, actual occupied penetration rates of those aged 75+ across the 30 largest metro markets varies from as low as 1 percent to as high as 11 percent. The average is about 4.8 percent.

"That delta between 5 and 13 percent is the opportunity for this industry over the next two decades," stresses Kramer.

Early in 2007, when the capital markets were fluid and the hedge funds active, a number of huge investment deals (Archstone-Smith acquired by Lehman Brothers and Tishman Speyer, Equity Office Properties bought by Blackstone) were completed just before the market turned sour. Seniors housing experienced one of those megadeals when Fortress Investment Group LLC bought Holiday Retirement Corp. for $6.607 billion.

The seniors housing investment market kept rolling through 2007. "I do a lot of mergers and acquisition work in the industry," says Gamzon. "I had been pushing along very happily doing $100 million to $200 million worth of business a year. In 2007, I personally did $695 million."

As with other real estate sectors, investment activity has all but withered away. In 2008, there has been very little investment activity, notes David Schless, president of American Seniors Housing Association. "Since the second quarter there has been very little deal flow."

So where does that leave seniors housing?

"The industry today continues to be healthy except for some individual markets. Florida and Las Vegas, where people can't sell their single-family homes, are facing challenges," says Schless.

He adds, whatever's in the pipeline will be built but after that there will be a limited amount of new construction.

If we break the near future into segments, the consensus is the industry will evolve in this manner: from 2008 to 2010, slowing construction, relatively healthy fundamentals, a strong focus on operations and not expansion; 2011 to 2019, the pace of new product development will pick up, just not enough to meet a growing demand, the introduction or expansion of a new generation of product, and more industry-wide consolidation; 2010 and beyond, the demographic factor kicks in with a vengeance.

CHAPTER EIGHT

THE CONDOMINIUM MARKET

Vacationland condos will bake empty in the sun a long time; Expect shorter, more moderate downturn for urban units

Back in 2005 during the heat of the condo boom, Richard Swerdlow decided to create an online marketing service for the condo investment community. He called it the Condo Exchange. But, the condominium craze began a rapid cooldown the very next year, and Swerdlow adroitly changed the focus of his web site, relaunching in mid-2007 as www.condos.com. It was a good move for Swerdlow, who a year later was calling his web site the "world's largest condo marketplace."

"When we launched, we had 6,000 listings, by spring 2008 we had 600,000 listings," he says. It seems everyone wants to get rid of their condo investment these days, and the Internet appears to be a good way to find a buyer—wherever that person may be in the world.

"At one time no one really needed a web site like www.condos. com," Swerdlow tells me. "There was such a demand for condos, developers would find people camping outside their condo projects to buy preconstruction units. Why did they need to advertise?"

That was not so long ago (2005), but it seems light years away from where we are today. Depending on the market, condo prices are falling faster than the down elevator in a high-rise condo project on Florida's Gold Coast.

"In a given market, prices have already dropped anywhere from 15 to 80 percent," Swerdlow observes.

That's the thing about condominiums: When it comes to valuation they exhibit a lot of volatility, much more so than a single-family residence.

Back in 2005, I wrote a story for *Urban Land* magazine, a publication of the Urban Land Institute, on what I called at the time, the condo bubble. Even then I could see the condo market was overbuilt and heading for a correction. I wrote: "Although there are condominiums that sell for seven figures and above, on a general level, condos sell for less than single-family homes. They are cheaper to buy, easier to rent if the owner doesn't want to live in the residence, and more subject to flipping (extreme short-term ownership). As a result, condo markets often exhibit a lot more price movement both up and down."[1]

In 2005, when I wrote that story, the condo market was raging. That year, almost 900,000 condo units changed hands in the United States. It was a peak year because by 2006, buyers started to back off and sales slowed. In 2007, volume dropped to 713,000 units sold and the estimate by the National Association of Realtors for 2008 was 560,000 units sold.

The tipping point for condos came in July 2007 when a record inventory of 731,000 of unsold condos was on the market, an 11.7-month supply, says NAR. About a year later, raw inventory had fallen to nearly 600,000 units. Inversely, that was a 13-month supply.

"We hear there are fewer new listings coming on the market, so that is good,"says Walter Molony, a senior associate with the NAR. "But the relative supply sits at a record high and that usually favors buyers. To have a rough equilibrium in the market between buyers and sellers you need to be at about a six-month supply."

In 2005, the month supply for condos was at 4.7 months, a market that favored sellers. The next year, the month supply rose quickly to 7.8 months as very suddenly the market began to favor buyers.

The percentage of sales declines was fairly uniform across the country, but value changes were very inconsistent across regions.

The NAR divides the country into four sections—Northeast, Midwest, South, and West—and each one began to react differently as the condo market cooled down nationally. In the West, prices began to collapse as early as 2006 and have dropped steadily since then, from a median price of $283,800 in 2005 to $241,000 early in 2008. In the South and Northeast, condo prices declined in 2006, rallied in 2007, and have been falling since then. Surprisingly, the strongest market has been the Midwest, which experienced condo price increases through 2007 before starting to decline. Also, condo prices in the Midwest haven't declined as quickly as other regions.

The NAR data illustrates the geographic disparity in regard to condo prices. In places such as Florida where feverish building and tremendous price appreciation were the order of the day, market shifts have been cataclysmic. In other areas of the country such as the Midwest, weaknesses have surfaced and prices are falling but at a very moderate pace and without marketplace panic.

"In the vast midsection of the country, from the Appalachian Mountains to the Rockies, markets have generally avoided wide (development and pricing) swings," says Molony. "Prices have increased at normal rates, up one or two points above inflation annually. Developers can meet demand because there are fewer land constrictions such as in large northeast cities."

Except in pricier mid-America markets such as Chicago, and maybe one other city like Minneapolis, opting to live in a condo was more a lifestyle choice because single-family residences are certainly affordable in those markets. In comparison, on the coasts and in other high-cost markets, condos initially became popular because they were more affordable than single-family homes. That was, of course, before the speculators hit the condominium markets and all hell broke loose.

Where We Were

The first explosion in condo construction began at the end of the 1970s and continued through the 1980s. It lasted less than a decade, screeching to a halt as a real estate recession settled across the country at the end of the 1980s.

Those were different times, because the condo boom back then came mostly at the lower end of the price scale. In the most recent boom, there were fewer lower-priced condos getting built due to higher construction costs and demand shifts within the market; luxury condominium development predominated.

The real estate recession of the late 1980s and early 1990s was the most severe in decades and really stopped condominium development cold. In 1996, for example, there was only one new condo project started in Miami-Dade County, Florida. In comparison, 12 years later, there were 15,000 more condominium units being built than were absorbed in that entire market during the years 1995 to 2004, reports Jack McCabe, a principal in McCabe Research & Consulting LLC in Deerfield Beach, Florida.

By the mid-1990s, a number of adventuresome investors began acquiring distressed properties, including condominiums, very cheaply. At the time there was really no modern precedent for what happened to real estate investments—especially condominiums—so despite prices hitting rock-bottom there was still a lot of risk in these investments.

Time healed most of the properties and that has affected today's market. Owners know that the prices will rise once again so they hold on to their properties longer, thinking they can wait this market out. But they won't be able to because the downturn in some areas, such as Florida, will be lengthy and prices won't come back until well into the next decade.

At some point, vulture buyers will help to stabilize the condo market because they understand the risk/reward equilibrium much better than in the past and will begin purchasing wounded investments.

"There is a lot more comfort with distressed property today than there was in the early 1990s," notes Matthew Anderson, a principal with Foresight Analytics LLC, an Oakland, California, real estate analysis firm.

Also, Anderson adds, the banks know better what to do with their bad investments. "In today's environment, there will still be foreclosures, but lenders looking at a defaulted loan are going to be reticent about taking on the headache of trying to complete an unfinished project and selling the units. They are more likely to turn around and sell the loan at a deep discount to a private equity investor, who would then take over the development."

Obviously, the banks are going to be saddled with huge losses on construction loans. Anderson suggests that what the banks are going to recover on a defaulted loan is going to be much lower today than in the past. Yet, that won't stop the loan unloading process. "The lesson banks learned from the 1980s and 1990s is that it is generally better to move nonperforming assets off the balance sheet as fast as possible and take the hit up-front. Those banks that delay will have to take the hit when commercial real estate begins to attract buyers and developers and they will get beaten up by the market," says Anderson.

If Anderson is right, a combination of factors should create a fairly fluid market for distressed condo properties in the next decade. Back in 2008, it just hadn't happened yet. Since the investment climate fairly screams out, "It is still too early to start buying," the begging question is "When will things change in the condo market?" The general answer is "Not anytime soon."

Where We Are Today

The condominium market is plagued by so many issues it's tough to get a bead on exactly how bad, or how good, it really is. Without any keen sense of where the floor is, investors won't invest and lenders won't lend. When nothing happens financially, markets don't stand still, they get worse.

The first problem confronting the condo market has to do with the overhang of construction that will haunt the industry at least through the beginning of 2009. Condominiums are a much different beast than single-family homes because condo projects have to be built on an all-or-nothing basis. You cannot build one or two condo units at a time; you have to do the whole building. If you're building a large-scale residential development and the market turns, you can end construction at the last house erected. However, if you are halfway through construction on a high-rise condo development and the market turns, you either complete the project and hope for the best or walk away and take a miserable beating—as will the lender.

Even in 2008, developers (and lenders) were still developing condo projects hoping to take a smaller loss selling the completed building rather than taking a big loss by just walking away.

The peak year for condo starts was in 2005, when 152 new projects got under way and 73 were completed, notes Foresight Analytics. Two years later, 120 projects were started and 117 were completed. In 2008, during the heart of the credit crisis and real estate slump, there were still 46 projects started and 88 were finishing up.

In hot markets gone cold, the forward momentum was so strong that even a market collapse couldn't halt new building. "In Miami-Dade County in 2008, about 19,000 condo units were scheduled to be completed," says McCabe. "Another 6,500 were slated to end construction in 2009."

In March 2008, Applied Analysis of Las Vegas charted over 24,000 proposed condo units that were canceled or suspended in that city. That still left 8,924 units under construction and an amazing 62,878 units still in the planning or proposed stage.

Since condominium values are very volatile, the asset often attracts a certain amount of speculative buying, although it's doubtful anyone predicted the bubble-icious craziness of the twenty-first century's first decade.

In Manhattan, for example, the number of condo sales jumped from 3,000 annually to 8,500 over the 10-year period of 1995 to 2004. During the same period the price per square foot for condos jumped from $250 to $800. In the first quarter 2008, the average price per square foot for a Manhattan condo stood at $1,416, reported Prudential Douglas Elliman Real Estate.[2] Although a steady influx of luxury condos skews these numbers upward, who wouldn't want to be in this kind of action: a couple of years living in Manhattan and then sell at a nice profit.

Although all condo markets have been driven to some degree by speculation, in Manhattan it is assumed most of those newly developed units are being lived in. What happened in Miami and the rest of Florida's coastal areas was something completely different.

Before the market began to turn, which was around the second half of 2005, a buyer could put a mere 5 to 15 percent down on a condo that wasn't yet built. So, for example, a buyer paid 10 percent, or $40,000, for a $400,000 unit in Miami, and there was such rampant inflation in regard to condo prices that by the time the building was completed two years later, the unit was now worth $600,000. Demand was so strong because the rewards appeared to be so great; people would wait in line to get into a new condo development. There were even lotteries on hot new properties.

The difference between Miami and Manhattan, says McCabe, was that the Florida market was driven by speculators who "never planned on living in these units; they were only in it for a quick profit."

Why Miami? For a vast spectrum of the population, from retirees and near-retirees to jet-setters and foreign investors, Miami was and still is a very desirable place to live.

"There were these incredible returns, which was why all the taxi drivers, housewives, lawyers, and doctors became real estate speculators," says McCabe. Then condo speculation fever spread like the plague across the land. In Las Vegas, Brian Gordan, a principal in Applied Analysis, reports 75 to 90 percent of the condo buyers in his city were purely investors or speculators who never intended to live in their investments.

All this speculation escalates pricing. Gordon explains what happened in his city: "Increased interest in Vegas as a condo destination attracted developers who began buying up land. We started to see land values literally doubling overnight particularly in the resort corridor. Investors were making a lot of money just on land plays, based on entitlements. Some had real plans for projects, others were just land speculators. So we had land prices jumping dramatically and that caused price points on the condo units to escalate. Because prices of units were also jumping, speculators were putting down deposits on two, three, five projects at a time."

The pace of sales was exaggerated relative to true demand—a common occurrence in overheated markets.

Where We Are Headed

Eventually the market catches up to reality and then the slaughter begins. In Miami, McCabe estimates that in a 12-month period from spring 2007 to spring 2008, condo prices declined 20 percent and that wasn't anywhere near a bottom.

That's a big problem. There is no apparent floor in pricing yet. What looks like a bargain today may not be because the value of your purchase could drop another 20 percent in a year. By the end of 2009, McCabe guesses prices will fall another 20 to 25 percent. He doesn't see any recovery until some time in the next decade.

There are a couple of ways to gauge how dysfunctional a market is and whether it is ripe for recovery or heading for more pain.

The most obvious indicator used today is the basic supply-demand equilibrium. Let's look at Atlanta, Georgia, as an example.

Using data produced by local real estate consultants Haddow & Company, the number of "active" projects increased from 95 in 2001 to a record 141 in 2007, which meant the number of units in Atlanta jumped from 7,363 to 13,032. Meanwhile, the percentage of those units closed or under contract dropped from a high of 62.9 percent in 2001 to an eight-year low in 2007 of 44.4 percent. If all that looks bad, you're right because unsold units totaled a record 7,252 in 2007, while annual condo unit sales dropped to 1,704, the lowest total since the turn of the millennium.[3]

Going into 2008, Atlanta was a city with annual condo sales declining while unsold condo units on the market were heading into the stratosphere. As with other cities, the spigot couldn't be turned off quickly enough and in 2008, more than 4,000 more condo units were added to the market. Already at the start of 2008, Atlanta condo prices dropped by 12 percent.[4] That's actually considered moderate. Condo prices in Tucson, Arizona, fell by 20 percent and in Cape Coral-Fort Myers, Florida, by 26 percent, notes the NAR.

Just as a frenzy of buying activity built up during the good years, which, in effect, amps up a market, just the opposite happens when a market bubble bursts. Negative actions create more pressure on declining prices. In the condo sector, these actions involve walking away from newly built condos and forfeiting down payments. Let's say a developer was very aggressive in bringing in buyers and he enticed an investor to acquire a $300,000 condo in Miami because she was a speculator and the amount of capital she needed to put up was just 5 percent, or $15,000. That's considered a sold unit. Then the market changes, and the value of the condo drops to $225,000. At that point, the speculator walks away.

With tight credit markets, an even worse situation has arisen. Some of those good folks who placed a down payment on a condo and really intended to live in it can't get financing. "If lenders continue to tighten up the mortgage requirements, mandating more equity, it will make it even more difficult for a buyer to close and units will fall out of escrow," says Gordon. As of 2008, there wasn't a great deal of that kind of thing happening, but that was because a lot of the new product was in the luxury category and buyers there generally have good credit and deep capital.

"The lending climate for condos in Florida is not so sanguine," says McCabe. "Lenders won't make mortgages on condos, especially in Miami-Dade County, because they fear if they make an 80 percent loan-to-value loan today, a year from now that note may be of greater value than the property because prices continue to drop and there would be no collateral to cover the debt."

McCabe claims some banks have established blacklists of condo projects around the country for which they will not make loans.

When a condo deal falls out of escrow, either because a bank won't make a loan or a speculator walks away, it means another condo is in the market to be sold. If enough buyers who made down payments walk away, developers will find themselves in deep financial holes, maybe too big to crawl out of. This is not an uncommon occurrence as the trend lines for construction loan delinquencies are heading in the wrong direction.

As of the third quarter 2003, construction loans outstanding in the condominium sector were still under $10 billion, notes Anderson of Foresight Analytics. Just over three years later, construction loans outstanding hit $45 billion and by the end of 2007 was still running over $40 billion a quarter. Even with that run-up, delinquency rates in the condominium sector averaged under 2 percent from the third quarter 2003 through third quarter 2006, and then it all fell apart. Over the next five quarters, delinquencies for condominiums rose to 2.6 percent, then 3.5 percent, then 4.2 percent, then 6 percent, before climbing above 10 percent in the fourth quarter 2007, says Anderson.

Judging from a supply/demand equilibrium, there's still a lot of pain left in the condominium market, and there has been little healing. In fact, the economic suffering is still being exacerbated by the credit crisis, escrow fallout, and rising loan delinquencies.

Another way to figure the instability of the condominium market is to look at the relationship of rental rates on apartments to condo expenses. In a balanced market, rental rates should equal 80 to 120 percent of what ownership costs are, says McCabe. In the fourth quarter 2006, a number of West Coast markets (Northern California, Los Angeles-Orange County, San Diego, Tucson, Portland-Beaverton, and Sacramento) showed the ratio of condo payments to rent are way over the 120 percent mark, but a year later three were back in an equilibrium range: San Diego, Sacramento, and Tucson, reports Foresight Analytics, so there has been some improvement, at least according to this particular metric.

A 2008 joint study by the Center for Economic and Policy Research and the National Low Income Housing Coalition observed, "As a ratio of sales price to annual rent of 15 to 1, ownership costs are roughly comparable to rents. At the peak of the bubble, the ratio of ownership costs to rents of comparable units crossed 20 to 1 and even 25 to 1." Using three metro examples from the study, the low-end New York metro area monthly ownership costs for residential hit $2,415, whereas the rental cost of a two-bedroom household came in at $1,318; in Los Angeles-Orange County, it was $3,054 in low-end ownership costs as compared to $1,300 for a two-bedroom rental; but in Dallas-Fort Worth-Arlington, it was $758 for low-end ownership versus $871 for two-bedroom rental.[5]

McCabe suggests two other tests to see whether a residential market has returned to normal. First, if household prices stand at three to four times the median household income, that should be a healthy market. In his state of Florida, the median household price remains at six and seven times, so, as he notes, "We are still way out of whack."

Finally, the last test rests on standard appreciation. Over the past 30 years, the average home appreciated 6 to 7 percent annually. Again, using Florida as an example, when the boom was on, appreciation hit 100 to 220 percent over a five-year span. At the same time household incomes only increased 2 percent. If one goes back to 2002, the start of the boom years, and figures 6 to 7 percent appreciation, that is how far home prices must come down before the state residential markets are stable again.

So when should investors start buying? The most optimistic estimate about condominium markets was by NAR's Molony, who predicts 2009 will see a return to normal conditions, but only in those markets that weren't skewed by speculative fever.

Anderson suggests the overhang of new construction will affect condo markets well through 2009. The time to consider buying is when construction starts grind to a halt, which doesn't look like it will happen until 2010.

McCabe, who lives and works in the Florida markets, expects a long ball game ahead. "We are in the bottom of the third inning, not the top of the ninth."

Bonus Box

Big Cities

Condominium markets in large, densely populated urban areas have been running on a different track than metros in Sunbelt areas that are popular as vacationlands and/or retirement destinations.

Through most of the twenty-first century's first decade, condo sales and pricing in Manhattan and Chicago remained strong despite what was going on in the rest of the country. Nevertheless, the effects of the economy and credit crunch (in Manhattan, layoffs in the financial sector) will take its toll, but the downturn will be moderate in comparison to places like Florida, San Diego, or Las Vegas.

In the first quarter 2008, the median sales price of a Manhattan apartment (condos and coops) hit $945,276, up 13.2 percent from the prior year. It was the first time the median sales price crossed the $900,000 threshold, although it was skewed by a number of closings at the high end of the market. While all that looked great, a couple of indicators suggest the Manhattan market was headed for a slowing. First, the number of sales in the first quarter was down 34.3 percent as compared to the same period the year before and down 9.4 percent as compared to the prior quarter. Second, the average number of days a Manhattan apartment was on the market increased, and third, just looking at condos, inventory levels in the first quarter jumped 11.1 percent.[6]

Chicago remains—by a very wide margin—the largest condominium market in the Midwest. Indeed, the Windy City is the third largest condo market in the country and in a striking note, condo sales in the nation's third largest city by population increased to 64 percent of all residential sales in 2008 as compared to 58 percent in 2006. As in Manhattan, a large part of downtown Chicago's intense skyline consists of high-rise condo buildings.

On the other hand, the cost of a Chicago condo is about a third of that in Manhattan. In March 2008, the median sales price was $312,000 and that was up 10 percent as compared to the same quarter the year before.[7]

By 2008, Mario Greco had been selling condominiums in Chicago for about six years. February of that year was his best month ever when he sold $22 million worth of properties, of which 75 percent were

Continued

(Continued)

condos. Greco is the lead broker of The Mario Greco Group within the larger Chicago firm of Rubloff Residential Properties, and in 2007 he was the number one condo resale agent in the Windy City. Even with all that activity, Greco sees the tide has begun to turn.

"Condo sales have been strong in Chicago for the last 10 years," he says. "Partly that has to do with Mayor Daly making the city livable and also because we have always had a strong job market in fields like law, finance, medicine, and education. Also, the demographics of Chicago were such that there was enough baby boomers who were becoming empty nesters and wanted to live in the city."

That was enough to carry Chicago through some tough years nationally for condo markets, but the party is finally coming to an end. The median sales price in March 2008 was basically even with the month before while the average time a unit was on the market jumped 16 percent.[8]

"We are seeing a slowdown in number of units sold," says Greco, but only to a level of a couple of years ago, which were then record years." Greco maintains there are two condo markets in the city, the downtown high-rise sector and the outlying Chicago environs, which are made up of smaller structures built on in-fill sites. He predicts a lull in the high-rise market as inventory begins to pile up. This period of relative quietude will last until the beginning of the next decade.

Even with a nascent inventory problem in the high-rise sector, Greco doesn't expect the market will give back much in terms of pricing. "Chicago's condo market was never driven by externalities such as the tech craze, the Vegas craze, Miami condo fever or any of that kind of stuff," he says. "It was never fueled by anything more than Chicago being a livable city and people like to live there. We have not seen stratospheric increases in values and we won't see a precipitous fall."

Block Condo Sales

Think of this as a trend delayed.

In November 2007, the Dow Jones Newswire ran a story about investors looking to dive into fractured condo projects in Florida by purchasing all unsold units in bulk. The actual term is *block condos*.

When I looked into this phenomenon near mid-year 2008, it was clear that the time was still too early for block condo sales. "By now we thought we would see some transactions, but we have not," notes

Brad Capas, a senior director of apartment-brokerage services at Cushman & Wakefield.

Even though Capas noticed a lot of buyers sniffing around, there were two huge impediments that had to be overcome—and weren't. The first was the liquidity problem. "If you are a bank, do you want to lend on something like this? Probably not," says Capas.

Second, block condo sales are done at very deep discounts. Developers and even owners of individual units had not yet felt enough pain to unload property so cheaply.

For Capas, the traditional thread of his job had been to sell apartment communities mostly to institutional investors, but in 2004, business started to shift to new buyers as condo converts hit the market big-time. For a while it looked like easy money for these developer/converters. The old investment model was for an investor to come in, buy an apartment community for, as an example, $80,000 a unit, hold for five to seven years, and sell for $95,000 a unit (plus rental increases of 3 to 4 percent a year). However, the condo converter would buy at $80,000 a unit, upgrade the community (cheaply!), then sell units at $130,000 to $150,000.

That cycle lasted about two years. In Florida, the condo conversion business started hitting the wall around 2005; eventually the rest of the nation followed suit. In Capas's definition, a fractured condo is one where the condo conversion was into the sale process, but the market changed and the developer was no longer able to sell the remainder of the units. Now some units are sold, some aren't, and the net result is a property that is worth less because it is considered broken, or fractured. It's hard to sell the existing units, and expenses run very high because costs aren't shared by many owners.

In 2008, the Real Estate Research Corp. (RERC) in Chicago estimated there were 500,000 units in busted (fractured) condominiums across the country which represented at least a several-year supply of units for sale based on condo absorption trends. Although many busted condos are still held by original developers, RERC was seeing more and more in the hands of lenders and basically all they want to do is liquidate the investment.[9]

A fractured condo is an "inefficient piece of real estate" with a lot of risk, says Capas, and although the present owner might have bought in at $80,000 a unit, the buyer of block condos will offer $40,000 to $50,000 a unit.

Continued

(Continued)

Why the lowball price? The buyer is looking to get a minimum return, let's say 15 percent, but buying the block condos cheaply still doesn't mean control of the entire project and the marketability of those condos being bought is uncertain.

Here's the way the strategy works. A 200-unit fractured condo had initially sold 50 units before the market went south. The investor offers to buy the remaining 150 condos at a discount. If the deal is completed, the new owner then offers a set price to buy out the remaining 50 unit holders. An aggressive buyer may present a fait accompli to the existing unit holders, saying, "I will buy the unsold units and all previously sold units, but every present owner has to sell or there will be no deal."

A couple of cautions for any investor interested in block condos, says Jules Marling, a partner and executive vice president with RERC. The first issue is control as condominium association documents typically have restrictions regarding the use of the property, which can prevent short-term rental. The second big issue is tax assessment because local assessors typically tag a condominium with a higher tax rate than a rental apartment. "In Florida, a normal tax rate on a rental might be $1,000 to $1,200 per annum," says Marling. "But, it wouldn't be unusual by applying the tax assessor's formula to come up with an assessment of $3,000 on the same space listed as a condominium."

In 2008, a number of opportunities for block condo investing surfaced, yet, as noted, little action occurred because the market was still going in the wrong direction. "Market timing is always difficult," says Marling. "Investors will need to wait it out."

The block condo owner will probably hold for five to seven years and then sell the whole project (returned to the rental market) to new investors. Or at some point in the future if the market blossoms again, he may attempt to do a second condo conversion.

In 2008, the main problem was lack of liquidity; the banks were just not funding this kind of risky investment. The backdrop was even more troubling, says Capas, with the whole condo market unsettled, still more buildings in the pipelines, vultures trying to buy defaulted loans, owners hoping foreigners will take up some of the empty units, no bottom on pricing, and no one really knowing which way it would turn. Says Capas, "It will be several years before the condo market sorts out and block condo investors start making deals."

PART

IV

OTHER ISSUES IN RESIDENTIAL REAL ESTATE

CHAPTER NINE

HOMEOWNER INSURANCE AND PROPERTY TAXES

Homeowners asked to carry a greater load;
No protection for coastal denizens

If you lived in Michigan for the last decade, as a homeowner, you faced a serious problem: The value of your home might be moving in the wrong direction. If you lived in Florida for the last decade, you also faced a serious problem. No, it wasn't the value of your home, which was steeply and steadily rising until the subprime crisis hit in 2007. The problem in Florida was the expense of owning a home there with the higher embedded cost of homeowner's insurance, if it could be gotten at all.

Over in Texas, where they often brag about having the biggest of everything, I've been told Texas homeowners pay the most in property taxes, at about an average rate of $1,250 to $1,300 annually per house, about twice the national average. However, Terry Butler, the insurance consumer advocate for the Florida Department of Financial Services, now tells me that Florida probably has passed Texas for that ignominious number one ranking.

Florida, Texas, and many areas along the Atlantic Coast and Gulf of Mexico have homeowner insurance problems: insurance costs increase, deductibles get bigger, and in some sections of the country with statistically high possibilities of severe weather damage difficulty in getting insurance at all.

For the rest of us, the cost of homeowner insurance has not hurt our pocketbook very much. In fact, some areas of the country might even have experienced a slight decline in cost.

"Over the last five years, outside of areas that have coastal exposure, homeowner's insurance premiums have been flat or decreased," says Robert Hartwig, vice president and chief economist with the Insurance Information Institute. "Nationally, there were general increases in the first part of this century, but for the past four to five years, outside of catastrophe-prone areas, any price increases have been very moderate."

Unless sometime in the next few years, tremendous losses are incurred by violent hurricanes or earthquakes, most of the country should not worry too much about homeowners insurance. It will rise at the pace of inflation and that's because rates are partly based on reconstruction costs and, needless to say, the price of everything from labor to materials has continued to climb.

"The cost of insurance will track the cost of building and repairing homes," says Butler. "The reality is, these costs rise over time, and insurance will have to incorporate those expenses into the price."

As a counterbalance to the rising prices, if the country passes quietly through the next few storm seasons, it is quite possible that homeowners will see insurance costs remain flat as carriers once again become competitive for market share.

"Away from the coast, homeowners insurance is in a fairly stable price period, because there were large increases between 2000 and 2003," confirms J. Robert Hunter, director of insurance for the Consumer Federation of America.

That rate increase was caused by the normal cycle of the industry. "Insurance companies go through periods of high profits where they intensely compete with each other, either leaving rates stable or cutting them," explains Hunter. "Then they get to a point where competition ends and everybody starts to jack up rates. This happens roughly every 8 to 12 years, depending on external influences such as interest rates and stock market movements."

Geographically, it would appear most of us are safe from escalating homeowner insurance rates, but in reality, the density of America's population sits along the coasts, and migration movements from colder to warmer climes, or suburbs to beach properties, means more of us are confronting insurance-adverse situations. This could mean serious repercussions for Americans like myself, who live in places like Arizona and never see a hurricane.

First of all, the impotence of states to control the cost of homeowners insurance might eventually upset migrations that have been established for decades. Second, in some places, like parts of Louisiana, the inability of homeowners to get insurance means they can't rebuild in townships—already devastated by a hurricane—that have traditionally been their homestead. Third, if the cost of insurance is too expensive, then retirees and young families get priced out of markets. In either case, insurance becomes an impediment to growth.

Fourth, a number of solutions are being floated to make home-ownership more affordable along the coasts and protect insurers in case of catastrophic situations. Any legislation adopted by the federal government will eventually affect all of us.

Where We Were

The common theory concerning insurance rate turmoil is that today's problems are directly linked to the busy and disastrous 2004–2005 hurricane seasons, where multiple storms, in particular Hurricane Katrina, pounded the Florida and the Gulf Coast areas. The insurance industry and homeowners were equally awash in problems after these storms, but the original sin happened in 1992 with Hurricane Andrew.

Until Hurricane Andrew, disaster models envisioned really terrible storms that would cause something like $4 billion to $5 billion in damages. Andrew caused $18 billion to $20 billion and sent shock waves through the insurance industry. When 1993 rolled around and it was time to renew insurance treaties, the reinsurers (who provide insurance to the insurers, allowing the latter to spread risk) excluded Florida. Without reinsurance, insurers weren't going to participate in the Florida market, so the state, as it should have done, stepped in and said it would provide the reinsurance.

Also, around 1994 to 1995, the insurers began to implement hurricane deductibles. Deductibles are very common in most types of insurance and it is usually a fixed amount, say $1,000 for fire loss. The hurricane deductibles became percentage-based. That type of deductible now exists in almost every coastal community in the country, generally at a minimum 2 percent figure. So if your home is worth $200,000 and it gets blown flat by a hurricane, the deductible, or money out of your pocket, comes to $4,000. If it burns down and you have a $1,000 deductible, money out of your pocket remains $1,000. (Some might carp there is a sense of unfairness here.)

So, after Andrew a couple of permanent changes hit the industry. States became involved in the insurance process for better or for worse. Second, insurers found a way for consumers to pay more for insurance, while reducing their risk.

To be fair to the insurers, one consideration about the deductible was that it would get people thinking about how they could control insurance costs by reducing exposure to hurricanes. In other words, if consumers are responsible for the first $4,000 of expenses after hurricane damage, it would provide an incentive to retrofit windows and doors, reinforce the roof, and so forth. How much of that actually happened is subject to debate.

Anyway, I came across two older newspaper stories with screaming headlines, "Home Owner Insurance Crisis to Worsen" and "The High Cost of Homeowners Insurance Sinks Home Sales." Both articles were written in 2002, and the country hadn't yet experienced the two terrible hurricane seasons of 2004 and 2005.

After Andrew, the insurers changed basic coverage to include this additional restriction, which almost nobody understood at the time, but made for great controversy after Katrina. "The most severe restriction was the anti-concurrent clause," which Hunter explains, basically said if you have two events roughly at the same time and one is covered and one is not, the insurers won't pay for either. Homes along the Gulf Coast were damaged by wind or flooding, but in many cases both. Wind is covered, but flooding is an optional, separate insurance, and many people didn't have it. Hence the insurers said, "We aren't insuring," and the homeowners, and/or state, sued.

"Homeowners insurance typically covers wind and water damage as long as it is not due to flooding," says Hartwig. "So if a roof gets blown off and water enters the house, that is covered. Flooding had never been covered in the history of homeowners insurance, and for the last 40 years the remedy has been the national flood insurance program, which offers coverage to virtually any homeowner in the United States at a subsidized rate. Unfortunately, many people, even those who could see the ocean from their windows, had not purchased flood insurance."

According to Hartwig, in 2004 there were 2 million homeowner claims from storms, and 2.3 million in 2005; Katrina alone produced 1.2 million claims. "Within two years of Katrina, only about 1 percent of the claims had been litigated or sent to mediation," he says. "The majority of claims were expeditiously settled."

Ah-ha, the insurers were good guys! Or maybe not.

"It's good for an industry to make money and to grow, but it's not good to make profits that are unreasonable," says Hunter. "We are at an unreasonable profit level in the homeowners insurance industry."

As Hunter views the industry, after Katrina, the insurers asked for large price increases, but "these were opportunistic rather than necessary." The national loss ratio for homeowners when Hurricane Andrew hit was 130 percent, says Hunter, which means for every dollar the consumer paid out, it cost the insurers $1.30. Hurricane Katrina was a much worse disaster in terms of total damage, yet the loss ratio was $0.75 for every dollar taken in from consumers.

"Insurers have raised their prices very high, cut coverage low, and a lot of damage was paid for by state pools (taxpayers rather than the industry), so insurers insulated themselves very well," Hunter maintains.

He adds a 2007 study by his organization, the Consumer Federation of America, reported record profits for property insurers in 2004 and 2005 despite significant hurricane activity. Profits in 2006 rose to unprecedented heights, with pretax profits likely to increase by over $30 million for property/casualty insurers, a jump from the previous record of more than $100 million for every man, woman, and child in America. Meanwhile, the amount that insurers paid in claims and expenses as a percentage of the premium collected in 2006 plummeted to a 50-year low.

The same study estimated retained earnings, or surplus, for the entire industry was $600 billion at the end of 2006 (2006 and 2007 were relatively quiet hurricane years in the United States). The largest loss ever suffered by the insurance industry, Hurricane Katrina, represents an after-tax loss of $26.3 billion, or just 4.4 percent of what was then the current surplus.

Where We Are Today: Insurance

Despite all those fine numbers, the property/casualty insurers still feel very insecure.

Three factors drive insurance premiums, notes Eric Goldberg, associate general counsel of the American Insurance Association. They are current period of increased hurricane frequency and severity, higher cost of labor and materials, and more people living in exposed areas.

The last of Goldberg's assertions is the tipping point. Immigration patterns and the rise of second-home markets in warm weather states continue to put more people in harm's way of most hurricanes that strike the United States. Over the past couple of decades the target market for homes in hurricane alleys has been more upscale, which inherently raises insurance rates. Since rates are nondiscriminatory for, say, a certain area, everyone pays the same percentage. Unfortunately, the effect of higher insurance percentages is in a sense discriminatory. Nouveau homeowners can afford the higher premiums even when their homes cost seven figures; older residents, often in cheaper housing, can't.

"If you bought a house 30 to 40 years ago for a modest cost, your house is probably worth multiples of what you paid for it, but you might not have any more cash than you did 30 to 40 years ago," says Goldberg.

Some states, and even the federal government, are considering granting subsidies to these good folks so they don't get priced out of their present homes. But, what happens if someone built a million-dollar house next to one of these older homes? How would a government policy subsidize one resident but not the other?

That's pretty much where we stand today. There's a lot of public policy debate about what to do about homeowners insurance, and it is tough to say how it will all settle out.

A lot of the battles are being fought in individual states. In 2003, lawmakers in Texas reworked the state insurance legislation so home insurance rates and premiums dropped by 13 and 9 percent on average, but that still leaves Texas as the most expensive, or second most expensive after Florida, for homeowners insurance.[1]

"The insurance industry would argue that Texas is a perilous state no matter where you live," says Alex Winter of Texas Watch, a consumer group, "and it's true we are always going to have higher rates than the national average because we have wildfires in West Texas, hail in North Texas, and hurricanes along the coast areas, but compare us to Florida, Louisiana, and California, states with a fair share of perils, and we are significantly higher."

Winter claims the insurance industry takes advantage of lax oversight in Texas. "Right on the heels of hurricanes Katrina and Rita, Texas rates started to dramatically increase and insurers pulled back from the coast," Winter says. "The insurers are always talking about the potential for insurance and catastrophic hurricanes. That's just the most recent of a long line of reasons they give us for charging us so much. Before hurricanes it was reinsurance, before that tort reform, and before that deregulation. They are still charging too much; hurricanes are the latest excuse."

Winter tells me, "Unless the Texas legislature steps in and takes real action, this will continue and will be harder for people to get quality insurance for the right price."

The trouble is, states often get involved in the property insurance quagmire and many of them just muck up the problem. For every South Carolina, which seems to have gotten it right, there's a Florida, a state in a world of insurance hurt.

Even the AIA's Goldberg praises South Carolina. "In 2006, the state enacted a package of legislative reforms that made sense," he says. "The state allowed carriers to set up pretax saving accounts, a lot like flexible medical accounts, to help fund deductibles, pay for storm shelters and generators. It's a market-based incentive program."

Goldberg concedes the state of Florida probably did the right thing back in 1993, when it stepped in to provide reinsurance, when the market turned dysfunctional after Hurricane Andrew. "That was 15 years ago," says Goldberg. "Lots of states have considered whether to create their own catastrophe funds since then and not one has done it."

That's probably because most state legislatures have looked at Florida and collectively have shaken their head in dismay. The state's Citizens Property Insurance Corp. provides 1.3 million Floridians with property insurance, becoming the largest homeowners insurance underwriter in the state. Still homeowners insurance is very expensive; it's difficult to get it in some coastal areas and the citizens are up in arms. On top of that, the program is underfunded.

"Their whole structure is really a house of cards," says Goldberg. "Florida says it provides $38 billion in coverage, but only has $3 billion in cash, so if a Category 3 hurricane hits Florida, causing $35 billion in losses, the state is going to have to run to Wall Street and get some bonds issued." Hopefully, when that happens, Walls Street will be functioning again.

If you think homeowners in Florida and along the Gulf Coast are the only ones suffering from higher homeowner insurance costs and inefficient state programs that would be a wrong assumption.

I had a long talk with Paula Aschettino, who out of frustration with rising homeowners insurance founded Citizens for Homeowners Insurance Reform. Aschettino lives on Cape Cod in Massachusetts.

Here's her story. When she moved to the Cape in 1998, her homeowners insurance was $1,300 a year. By 2003, it had risen to $1,800. Today, it stands, for the moment, at $4,300. "I have a big old house and my policy represents $650,000 in replacement costs, but I have to pay the first $13,000 if there is wind damage," she tells me. "Sometimes I wonder why I have insurance."

Insurance companies, both private and the state's very own FAIR plan, increased wind deductibles for homes on the Cape and the nearby islands, including Nantucket, from 3 to 5 percent of face value. "Everyone thinks people who live in these areas are wealthy, but there are a lot of people who have smaller homes, with a replacement value of, say, $400,000. At a 5 percent deductible, those people are responsible for the first $20,000 of wind damage."

The problem in Massachusetts is that the state has had to jerry-rig an old program called the Massachusetts FAIR plan, which was established in 1968 as an insurer of last resort for urban areas.[2]

"The FAIR plan was formed when there was a lot of race riots in the cities and insurance companies did not want to insure where there were fires, and so forth," Aschettino explains. "But in order to rebuild the inner cities, there needed to be insurance. The FAIR plan was the insurance of last resort."

Today, the FAIR plan is the only insurer for over 40 percent of homeowners on Cape Cod and the Massachusetts islands.[3]

"We have a crisis in this area," Aschettino says. "Our seniors, who are on fixed incomes, are suffering because the payments here have gone up so high. They are either taking money out of their retirement to fund insurance payments or have dropped insurance.

They will probably sell when the real estate markets pick up because they can no longer afford insurance."

Where We Are Headed

There was one other change after Hurricane Andrew that was not so apparent. Insurers have to file their rates in the various states and in doing so, submit all kinds of information to state insurance commissions to get approvals to charge the rates they want. Prior to Hurricane Andrew, the concept of reinsurance as a factor or part of the rate submission process by an insurance company was rare; most of the information filed was related to catastrophic loss. "What ended up happening," explains Dennis Burke, vice president of state relations for the Reinsurance Association of America, "was a number of companies started to feel squeezed because insurance departments were not permitting them to get what they believed to be an adequate rate for catastrophic risk, that there was a disconnect between what the private reinsurance market was charging for risk and what they were able to get in their rate filings."

All this consternation resulted in insurers getting state laws changed, permitting them to include reinsurance costs in their rates. Thus, reinsurers also got to be part of the blame game.

The old hurricane catastrophic loss models underestimated Hurricane Katrina by 50 percent, says Burke, so when new models were created boosting loss expectation, there was a sudden demand for reinsurance. "Around 2006, demand for reinsurance outstripped supply; prices rose. When prices go up, capital comes in and $43 billion of capital entered the reinsurance field and prices started to moderate," says Burke.

What is the forward trend line? Again, unless another awful weather year like 2004 or 2005 occurs, reinsurance prices will continue a moderate ride on a downward slope.

Okay, things look good for reinsurance going forward. Does this mean homeowners insurance costs will drop? Probably not. That will only come when the insurers stop being fearful and start becoming competitive again in regard to signing up consumers, and there is no indication that will happen in the near future.

At this point in a chapter, I usually indicate where the markets will be headed going into the next decade. First of all, there doesn't seem much improvement ahead because the insurers are still trying to cut their downside risk, although some would say they are about as risk protected as possible and certainly do have the reserves in case of another big storm. Second, if there is another bad hurricane year, or major earthquake in California, then the insurers will undoubtedly go through another period of consternation, and look for new ways to cut risk, which could only mean even higher rates for people living along the coasts.

As noted, various government entities, both federal and state, are looking for ways to control homeowners insurance. Growth cannot occur when insurance becomes an impediment to expansion. If the common folk are taking more money out of their wallets to pay for insurance, that means dollars are not being spent elsewhere in the economy.

So, instead of saying this is where the homeowners insurance market is headed, I'm going to mention a few good ideas that have been proposed and if adopted might go a long way to ameliorating what is a very serious issue.

While researching homeowners insurance, I came across a press release from the office of Congressman Charlie Melancon (D-LA). The headline read, "Rep. Melancon Tackles High Cost of Homeowners Insurance in Coastal Louisiana." I gave him a call.

He told me in some regards he was very lucky. Hurricane Katrina blew east of his home, Hurricane Rita blew west. In the two storms, he lost one shingle. That didn't make much difference to insurers, because his homeowners insurance jumped from $1,700 a year to $4,500 with a $5,000 deductible and a 5 percent deductible on storms. Total replacement value of his house is $300,000, so if it does get flattened by a hurricane, he pays the first $15,000.

That's better than some in Louisiana who found out after the storm that they weren't insured, because damage was done by flooding—the old controversy, which came first: wind or water? And if there's no insurance, homes don't get rebuilt.

Melancon has thrown his support to various bills that support the concept of states joining together to pool catastrophic risk funds. For example, the Homeowners Defense Act, introduced in 2007, would have allowed states to responsibly plan for disasters ahead of time, while providing emergency relief for states located in lower-risk regions. Essentially, the bill provides a venue for state-sponsored insurance funds to voluntarily pool catastrophic risk with one another, and then transfer that risk to the private markets through the use of catastrophe bonds and reinsurance contracts.

I wasn't sure why other states would want to pool with Louisiana or Florida, but I like the concept, because one year Tampa, Florida, might be hit by a storm, and the next year Charleston, South Carolina. In either event, there would be enough coverage by the cojoined, state-sponsored insurance pools to adequately cover the damages.

The AIA's Goldberg suggested to me a very sensible idea of allowing insurers the ability to price their product in a way that actually reflects risk. What he was referring to is getting the local municipalities and states to enforce building codes as a way to keep homeowners out of harm's way, and then insurance can be tied to a home's ability to withstand a storm. "Some states have very weak building codes or no building code enforcement," exclaims Goldberg. "How can you let people build on a coast if you will not require them to build to a standard that will make sure their house is standing after a hurricane? Enforcing building codes is the key."

This is a very commonsense idea, and some states have already imposed building standards for homes in hurricane-prone areas. I would think we should see more of this type of legislation.

Finally, one idea, which is an extension of the building code concept, came from Florida's Butler. He suggests that a structure's vulnerability to catastrophic loss be made known at the time of sale. Today, even in Florida, there is barely any kind of hurricane strength rating on a house, but the buyer certainly knows if the home has granite countertops or hardwood floors.

When you buy a car, you know the fuel-efficiency and rollover ratings, plus all the other safety features. Well, why not do the same with homes? A house that is retrofitted to withstand a Category 5 hurricane should sell for more than a house that is not—and it should require less insurance.

As Butler says, "You cannot drive a car off a lot without having insurance, but you can build a house, get a certificate of occupancy, and get pretty far along in a house transaction before you investigate the cost of insurance."

Where We Are Today: Taxes

"Florida has some dynamic problems with insurance and property taxes," notes Jack McCabe, CEO of McCabe Research & Consulting in Deerfield Beach, Florida. "We are in hurricane alley, and insurance costs about $12,000 a year, and add another $8,400 for taxes. The latter is based on an average 2.2 percent home value."

At the end of 2006, a group called Florida TaxWatch issued a report that began this way: "Florida's property tax system is in crisis." The report listed numerous problems, but focused on two: actual property tax levies were skyrocketing and a state constitutional amendment called "Save Our Homes," a form of homestead tax relief, created a host of new problems and solved few.

I'll briefly mention the homestead problem first, which the report said, shifted billions of dollars in taxes from some taxpayers to others each year, created inequities in tax treatment, increased housing costs for renters and new home buyers, and restricted the financial ability of some people to move to a different home.[4]

Even with all of that, the chief problem in Florida still falls to skyrocketing levies, which were a direct result of the boom in home prices. The local communities haven't increased the tax rate, called the mill rate, but even doing nothing, escalating property values created a windfall of tax revenues for cities, counties, and school districts.

A similar problem occurred in the 1970s, the era of tax revolts, and resulted in Proposition 13 in California. The California tax revolt movement often cited the fact that older Californians were being priced out of their homes by high taxes, a problem some states, like Florida, try to solve by passing "homestead" provisions, but keeping the same tax rate.

States, counties, and local municipalities provide services, which are paid for by taxes of one sort or another. If they reduce one, they raise another.

"The state will get your money some way," says Natalia Siniavskaia, the author of a property tax report for the National Association of Home Builders. "If you pay lower property taxes, you end up paying a higher sales tax or income tax."

There are two ways to look at property taxes. The NAHB report came out in 2005 and using median value of homes as a baseline, showed New Jersey as the state with the highest real estate taxes followed by New Hampshire, Connecticut, New York, Rhode Island, and Massachusetts. A second way is to use the measure of median real estate taxes per $1,000 value of a home, and in the NAHB report, Wisconsin is number one, followed by Texas, Nebraska, Vermont, and New Hampshire.

"Traditionally, the South lowers property taxes, but New England relies heavily on property taxes," says Siniavskaia. "While Texas is high in property taxes per $1,000 value of home, you don't pay income taxes in the state."

When California imposed Proposition 13 to reduce real estate taxes, impact fees rose. Which is better? Elliot Eisenberg, NAHB's senior economist, argues that impact fees actually raise the price of homes, but real estate taxes reduce it. "If we raise impact fees, that means the builder has to pay higher fees and that gets passed on to the buyer," he explains. "The price of the home has to increase because the developer will not absorb those costs. When you raise the price of new homes, the prices of existing homes get lifted at the same time."

On the other hand, let's say that a certain percentage of the population can only pay X amount for a house in Sarasota, Florida, but if real estate taxes are added to the equation, homes now cost X plus taxes. To make the homes affordable to the people who want to buy in Sarasota, you actually have to reduce the price so the cost of the homes plus taxes equals that X amount. Hence, raising property taxes reduces the value of a house.

"Nobody likes property taxes," stresses Gerald Prante, an economist at the Tax Foundation. "It's necessary, but despised."

As in Florida, what has happened in most states is that property values increased very fast, but local governments are not lowering the tax rate to compensate, so taxes continue to rise. "From 2002 to 2005, property taxes were one of the fastest-growing revenue sources for governments," says Prante.

He adds, "If you want to cut taxes, you basically have to cut government spending." Since governments rarely cut spending, they raise other taxes.

No matter how one measures property taxes in the Sunshine State, the much-maligned Florida ranks in the middle of the pack. As noted, the grievances people have in Florida were due—at least until mid-2007—to stampeding home values. Citizens in Florida shouldn't complain too much; there is no state income tax.

Florida is one of a number of states with homestead provisions, which protects a percentage of a taxpayer's average home value from taxation. Usually this provision is reserved for the poor or elderly. The design flaw in original homestead provisions means that if an elderly person sells his or her house to move to a new house, the next residential abode is taxed heavily, so those who have the homestead advantage cannot afford to move elsewhere.

The way to make a homestead provision work better is to make it portable, allowing the tax protection to function in at least one new move. Portability for homestead provisions will probably prevail in those states with such legislation.

Also going forward, two mini-trends in regard to property taxes have been picking up speed, notes Bert Waisanen, a senior fiscal analyst at the National Council of State Legislatures. First is direct, quick, and targeted tax relief to sets of the population, usually seniors, people on fixed income, and lower-income homeowners. The second involves more structural reform, says Waisanen. States that are reducing property taxes generally are increasing the reliance on sales taxes to fund schools and other services.

The citizenry doesn't like property taxes because they consider them taxes on ownership and wealth, Waisanen observes. "The sales tax is broad based and everybody—consumers, businesses, even tourists—within the economy participates. Besides, it is more difficult to do a property valuation (for tax purposes) than to just slap a 5 percent sales tax on potato chips and candy."

Bonus Box

Halfbacks

Back in 2007, I was interviewing a news source in Atlanta, when he threw the word *halfback* into the conversation. It struck me as odd because I only knew the word in reference to football. In fact, I used to play halfback on my high school football team, but I'm an original baby boomer so I'm sure it's an outdated term today.

Anyway, I had to stop the conversation and ask exactly what he was referring to when he used the word, and I was surprised to learn it had an exact, nongridiron meaning. The term refers to retirees or near-retirees from the Northeast who moved to Florida but didn't like it, and moved halfway back to the Northeast, resettling in a narrow band of states: Georgia, South Carolina, North Carolina, and eastern Tennessee.

On the East Coast, the halfback phenomenon has garnered a lot of publicity, and I knew it was a trend line that needed to be mentioned in this book. But, here's the odd thing. There might actually be more smoke than fire. "Since there's no national survey that looks at people's migration history, there's no way to verify the halfback phenomenon," avers Charles Longino, the director of the Reynolda Gerontology Program and professor of sociology at Wake Forest University. In fact, Longino doubts such a trend exists.

On the other hand, Don Bradley, a professor of sociology at East Carolina University, says his state receives a lot of halfbacks, which he says are older folk, who are now making their secondary move, after an initial migration to Florida. He refers to it as the I-95 phenomenon. Seniors and near-retirees from New York to Philadelphia move south down the I-95 corridor to Florida, then come back up I-95 halfway back to the Northeast.

The reason retirees move out of Florida has to do with, first, the bad hurricane seasons of 2004 and 2005, and second, the increased cost—insurance and taxes—of living in the Sunshine State. They move north to beach/resort areas like Hilton Head, South Carolina, or try something different like mountain communities around Asheville, North Carolina, and Gatlinburg, Tennessee.

Actually, I have firsthand experience of the Florida move-out trend. My great aunt retired to South Florida around the turn of the millennium but after living through multiple hurricanes in 2004 and 2005, she moved away—not to the halfback region, but all the way to Las Vegas. I guess she figured there would be no hurricanes in Nevada.

Although both Bradley and Longino concede the halfback phenomenon is more empirical than scientifically measured, folks in the four-state halfback zone firmly believe in it. I came across a web site called floridahalfbacks.com, which boasted "mountain and lake destinations for Floridians," and, indeed, it was marketing the Appalachian Mountain regions of east Tennessee and west North Carolina.

The research is still exploratory, says a source at the web site, but they detect a decline in the number of "older folk" moving to Florida and an increase in those moving away. "What portion is directly related to hurricanes or increased living costs is hard to say," says the source.

There is one other theory to the halfback phenomenon, if it does exist.

Retirement and tourism destinations today must offer a variety of sun experiences, from beach to golf to recreational and cultural amenities. On the East Coast, Florida was the earliest state to offer

Continued

(Continued)

these experiences and came to dominate the market. Now, however, many places along the East Coast can offer similar programs, plus an added feature: scenic mountains. In essence, the retiree market is becoming decentralized, and Florida will increasingly have to share with other good beach locales. The knee-jerk move is Boca Raton, but it's hard to keep them down in the Sunshine State when they've discovered less crowded locales such as Sea Island, Georgia, or Daniel Island, South Carolina.

CHAPTER TEN

URBAN AND SUBURBAN INFILL

Sudden leap in gas prices gives impetus to new urbanism concepts; Much woe to new developments on the fringe

Back in late 2007 when I was organizing this book, I decided to add a chapter on urban infill. This is a concept that came to life in the 1980s and then gathered momentum behind a couple of intellectual movements in the 1990s called new urbanism and smart growth.

My sense at the time was that while infill development in urban locations had definitely picked up steam during the past decade, in some ways the low- or no-down mortgage rate phenomenon had actually worked against it, promoting instead cheap single-family development further out on the exurban fringe.

By 2008, as I was in the throes of writing the book, events actually overtook me in regard to the whole patchwork of development called urban infill. The difference between late 2007 and mid-year 2008 was the rapid rise in the price of gasoline. From June 2007 to June 2008, gasoline prices climbed 26 percent and the average price of gasoline hit $4 a gallon for the first time in the country's history.[1]

Gasoline prices had been climbing steadily for decades. In 2004 prices at the pump passed the $2 a gallon level. The cost then accelerated until 2008 when the speed of price increases moved forward faster than we could stuff our wallets with greenbacks. It seemed unheard of that the price of crude oil would reach $100 a barrel, but in mid-year 2008 crude was trading at over $140 a barrel.

The general feeling among economists was that Americans might have reached the tipping point in regard to making lifestyle adjustments to the high cost of fuel. The term *tipping point* was much publicized by journalist Malcolm Gladwell in his book of the same name, which essentially means the moment when a slow gradual change becomes irreversible and then quickens.

Economists were predicting that the high cost of gasoline had finally reached a point where it would change our driving habits and that eventually Americans would factor in the cost of commutation when considering where they might live in the future. In other words, new developments on greenfield sites, further out farmlands, and open ranges would become less desirable, while denser infill developments would attract tomorrow's homeowners.

All this will take time to happen.

"Faced with higher gas costs, people will change their behavior. That is the easiest thing to do in the short term," notes Gary Engelhardt, an economic professor at Syracuse University's Center for Policy Research and author of the 2006 research paper "Study of Housing Trends among Baby Boomers." "They will change their driving patterns, car pool, drive less or buy a hybrid instead of an SUV. These decisions will happen at a higher frequency than changing home buying decisions."

Back in 2006, Engelhardt's study exploded a myth that baby boomers were moving back to urban cores in large numbers. As he says, "In fact, baby boomers were just as likely to move to another suburb as they were to move back to an urban area."

Just two years later, Engelhardt says, "All bets are off."

Baby boomers haven't changed their attitude about urban living, he says, but there is a new reality in higher gas prices and that will change everyone's attitude to where they live. "We are going to have denser cities," he predicts. "With no prospects of gas prices falling, this will signal the demise of the bedroom community where people are commuting long distances. You will see denser metro areas around employment centers."

Engelhardt wasn't just talking about city centers. The new urbanism of today is not just urban infill, but suburban infill, mixed-use redevelopment of existing structures surrounded by huge surface parking lots, transit hub development, and the development of new communities that will have retail, office, and residential all planned together.

Where We Were

"The new urbanism and smart growth movement started in the early 1990s in terms of people coming together to articulate some alternatives to the sprawl that had gotten out of control by the 1980s and early 1990s," recalls David Goldberg, communications director for Smart Growth America. "We were consuming land at the rate of three times the population growth."

The idea behind new urbanism was to reexamine how we develop, to figure out where population growth was moving, and to some extent control what was to be built. Eventually, new urbanism got confused with no-growth and anti-growth efforts, but that was not what the concept was all about, so a new theory emerged called Smart Growth.

"This came out of a difference impulse," says Goldberg, "which was, let's assume the growth is going to happen, but instead of stopping it, let's try to shape it more consciously and involve the communities in thinking about how things should look, what landscape needs to be conserved, where infrastructure should be built."

All these concepts got an added boost by two unrelated factors. First, the Generation X cohort made a difference. Unlike the baby boomers, many Gen Xers delayed having children, delayed getting married, were strongly work oriented, but they also sought exciting lifestyles such as cities offered.

While population movements appear abstract, they actually are reflected in our cultural pastimes. For example, during the 1950s and 1960s when families embraced the suburban ethic, popular television shows like "Leave It to Beaver," "Donna Reed Show," "Ozzie & Harriet," "Father Knows Best," and many others were located in some amorphous suburban locale, but starting in the 1990s and into this first decade of the twenty-first century, popular and/or cutting edge shows such as "Cheers," "Friends," "Seinfeld," and "Sex in the City" were all about the city life.

Around the same time, many of America's cities actually became better managed, were cleaned up, crime was reduced, and redevelopment slowly improved the surroundings and brought housing back to inner cities or near inner cities.

Goldberg uses Atlanta as an example. "No one really lived in downtown Atlanta," he says. "But, with the advent of the 1996 Summer Olympics, some developers used the Olympic's financing potential to convert existing commercial buildings to residential. When that proved successful, they started to build new buildings. Then the midtown district just north of downtown took off like a rocket."

Using U.S. Bureau of the Census numbers, the Urban Land Institute came up with some interesting statistics. Between 1990 and 2000, most major U.S. cities experienced healthy population increases: New York (+9.4%), Houston (+19.8%), Chicago (+4%), Dallas (+18%), San Francisco (+7.3%), Boston (+2.6%), Memphis (+6.5%), Columbus (+12.4%), and San Antonio (+22.3%). In fact, of America's top 20 cities by population, only four experienced population loss: Philadelphia (−4.3%), Detroit (−7.5%), Baltimore (−11.5%), and Milwaukee (–5%).[2]

The urban movement continues unabated, although through the early part of this first decade, a counter drift occurred, mostly fueled by the advent of low interest rates, no-down and low-down mortgage loans and a policy of the federal government and government-sponsored enterprises (GSEs) such as Fannie Mae and Freddie Mac to push homeownership. As a result of these factors, builders swept up huge tracts of land beyond the last suburb and began building massive developments.

"With irrationally low interest rates, everyone climbed aboard the homeownership train and infill fell off the radar screen," observes Douglas Bibby, president of the National Multi Housing Council. "Everyone was trying to get as many people into single-family housing as they possibly could. Policy makers and the media were just beating this drum. Infill fell out of favor and we ended up chewing up more and more green space, pushing the boundaries of our suburbs out as far as they could go and creating isolated communities and very long commutes."

Where We Are Today

Those long commutes are now coming back to haunt us—and emptying the wallets of those new homeowners who saw cheap housing 40 miles from the big city as a way to live the American dream.

In 1983, the average U.S. commuting distance to work was under nine miles; but by 2001, the distance stretched to 12 miles.[3] Increased distances seemed to be acceptable when gasoline was still relatively cheap. Once gas prices jumped to $3 then $4 a gallon, we hit a tipping point. (By the end of 2008, gasoline dramatically declined once again, but the psychology of high energy prices didn't.) From January 1, 2008, through mid-year 2008, demand for gasoline fell 1 percent, according to the Department of Energy, which indicates 2007 will represent the peak year of gasoline consumption with annual demand dropping in 2008 for the first time in 17 years.[4]

Assuming some of this lack of fuel consumption is due to commuters slacking off on car use, how are they getting to work? Anecdotal evidence shows a number of cities reporting increased use of mass transit. In the Phoenix/Mesa area, where I live, a notoriously sprawling metropolis, ridership on commuter lines rose 8.5 percent in January 2008, 6.8 percent in February, 15.9 percent in March, and 17.9 percent in April.[5] A headline in a May 30, 2008, issue of the *Wall Street Journal* screamed, "Riders Swamp Public Transit."[6]

It's fortunate the new urbanism concept gained traction in the 1990s, because a number of cities across the country, including Phoenix, have been building up light-rail systems as a means of moving people about without their having to jump into their automobiles and waste energy. If people want to forsake their cars, these cities are ready to transport them.

In regard to real estate, new public commuter trains and light-rail systems engendered a subset of smart growth that called for the construction of denser, mixed-use developments around transportation nodes such as light rail or commuter rail lines. These new developments weren't aimed for downtowns per se, but near downtown locations and in suburban locations where the rail lines came through. By making these nodes of development denser and mixed-use, more people could reach their basic shopping stores by foot plus commute to employment.

Also in the 1990s, smart developers eschewed the bedroom community (just homes) concept and began to build new communities that included single-family residential, multifamily, retail, and office. The concept proved so successful that owners of shopping malls began rethinking their properties, especially the older malls surrounded by acres of flat parking. By converting these properties to mixed-use developments with the addition of multifamily and small office, they were increasing density, making better use of land and improving the retail efforts.

For the past 30 years, corporations would choose a greenfield site somewhere in the exurbs and build a plant, knowing that development would follow. This paradigm doesn't work well anymore, and it certainly won't work in the future with the cost of gasoline so uncertain.

"The structural element in the cost of fuel is significant and permanent and this will have an effect on corporate location decisions," says Jay Biggins, executive managing director of Biggins Lacy Shapiro & Co., a specialty site selection and incentives advisory firm. "In our business, we are already seeing commutation costs as a variable in corporate location decisions."

Access to the corporate facility has always been a location variable but now it increasingly has become a variable focused on mass transit access. "If companies believe employees might change their behavior in terms of commuting decisions, they will put a plant at a mass transit hub instead of at the intersection of Interstates Y and X, 30 miles outside the city," says Biggins. "You are going to see more mixed-use developments, more work and play environments. Companies like transit hubs for office locations."

The two predominant trends during the 1990s and into this first decade of the new century were "edgeless cities": (1) the urban hub connected by a freeway or high-speed arterial and (2) walkable urban.

Researchers report there is a 50-50 split between those who want drivable suburbs and those who want walkable urban, notes Christopher Leinberger, director of the University of Michigan's real estate graduate studies and a Visiting Fellow at the Brookings Institution, a Washington, D.C., nonprofit public policy organization.

The problem, Leinberger adds, is that the supply of walkable urban is just 5 to 10 percent of all housing.

"Walkable urban is expensive housing because there is a mismatch between supply and demand," he explains. "The price premium between walkable urban and drivable suburban is often 40 to 200 percent."

The difference in price can be laid to a number of infrastructure factors. First, the walkable urban housing is usually high density, which means it is a better built product with reinforced concrete, structural steel, and so on, as opposed to stick-built housing in the suburbs. Secondly, the price of land is more expensive because often there is just not a lot of it available.

This is where the economics of construction go haywire. On a per unit basis, the cost to build out infrastructure is much more expensive in the suburbs. To lay in a sewer line costs relatively the same amount of money whether done in a city or the suburbs. However, the cost in the burbs would be spread out over one or two units per acre, whereas in the city, it would be spread out over 40 to 80 units per acre. Although the infrastructure costs are so much higher in the suburbs for such things as sewer, water, electricity, schools, parks, public safety, and so on, citizens in the city pay the same amount for these government-regulated services as do the folks in the burbs. The folks who live in the suburbs are in effect being subsidized, says Leinberger.

The reasons why housing has gone haywire, says Leinberger, are (1) we have a de facto domestic policy that encourages and mandates low-density, surburban development through subsidies; (2) most jurisdictions have regulations that forbid high-density, walkable developments; and (3) for the last 15 years Wall Street only wanted to finance developers that built drivable suburban product.

Demographics

As with other housing sectors, whether it is second homes or vacation homes, the issue of new urbanism needs to be discussed in the general realm of demographics.

"Back in the 1950s and 1960s, about half of American households had children," observes Arthur C. Nelson, Presidential Professor at the University of Utah and director of its Center for Metropolitan Research. "That percentage dropped to one-third in the 2000 census and has since come down to a little above 25 percent and has stabilized there. That means that starting in the next decade, three-quarters of households won't have children."

That's because they already raised their children and are living longer or they have not yet raised children. But the majority of housing constructed in America from the 1950s through the 1970s was for households with children.

"The huge cohort called the baby boomers will live longer than prior generations," says Nelson, "and we know from various residential surveys if the boomers have a choice between near a downtown and the far suburbs, just 19 percent choose suburbs. Suburbs were not designed to cater to their (aging boomers) needs. Surveys show that downtown and closer-in developments are attractive to 50 percent of the baby boomers, while 30 percent prefer planned communities."

At the other end of the housing spectrum, the next large cohort to come into the market is called the millennials or echo-boomers, who are now coming out of colleges and universities into the job market and will do so for the next 15 to 20 years. The household dynamic will continue to change, says NMHC's Bibby, with single heads of households, unrelateds living together, and singles living independently. "By 2010," Bibby adds, "one in five households will be a married couple with children."

Until 2006 when the housing slump hit, there were two trend lines moving in opposite directions, and one is being played out, avers Smart Growth's Goldberg. "We had this machine that was revved up for commodity subdivisions on the fringe that was packaged and traded by Wall Street. It was our affordable housing for the last decade. At the same time there were developers trying to figure out how to do profitable infill development. The movement of people who would go out and buy a piece of farmland, with no regulation on it, and carve it into subdivisions is played out due to a conversion of forces."

The old subdivisions were built for the baby boomers and their children, says Goldberg. "They are no longer looking to harvest another crop of homes in the suburbs. While yes, some may want to retire to a mountaintop, others want to be closer to services."

Where We Are Headed

For much of the George Bush administration, the emphasis was on homeownership and in some ways the Federal Reserve's low interest rate policies and the financial system's engineering of mortgage products all supported the concept. Most of all, the home builders took advantage of all that to buy up huge swatches of land and mass-produce ever more housing.

People who are losing homes today direct their anger at the banks and the governments. Research analysts, university professors, and urban theorists place the blame on the developers and the financial systems that support them. "The people who need to be taught a lesson are the developers," explains Nelson. "The market is there for a walkable product. They don't build it because it is more difficult. Unlike drivable suburban where you can build a house and market it, with walkable urban you are building a place that has to be approximate to a rail stop or a Trader Joe's and with something like a festival that happens every weekend. It's harder to create that than build a stick-built home in the middle of nowhere."

One sector of the development industry that seems to have gotten the message is the multifamily builder, who has started to focus less on suburban garden-style apartments and more on downtown mixed-use and transit-oriented products. This isn't to say that apartment builders are forsaking the suburbs; they aren't, because there are still a lot of employment bases in the burbs.

"The bottom line is, when you look at your cost to develop a downtown high-rise and transit-oriented product, your construction costs are going to be so much higher versus a suburban stick-built project," explains Matthew Lawton, senior managing director of the Chicago office of Holliday Fenoglio Fowler LP. "So, the rents you are going to have to achieve to make the return thresholds on urban and transit-oriented are much higher."

The land for urban and transit-oriented product is more expensive as well, but Lawton predicts that one of the key trends over the next decade will be the tearing down of older apartment complexes constructed in the 1960s and 1970s that are functionally problematic, waste a lot of land, and are relatively close to urban centers.

"We will see a lot of these older, functionally obsolete projects being scrapped and redeveloped into three- and four-story buildings with structured parking, much denser unit count, and more efficient 'amenitized' units," says Lawton. "A lot of these older projects were built 40 years ago on the fringe of the cities or in early suburbs but are now infill."

Cities will be happy to see this happen, because not only are older, worn-out projects being replaced, but municipal governments, which are always looking for more revenue, will have a property that had been 10 units to an acre and is now 20 to 25 units to an acre that has increased in value, thus creating a larger tax base. In addition, the quality and demographic of the renters change as well.

"Realistically, only about 1 percent of the population wants to live in an urban downtown," says Nelson, "with 5 percent wanting to be near downtown, accessible to downtown, or near a transit node, and 25 percent preferring a suburban downtown or multiuse planned community."

"Just to meet the demands of that 30 percent of the population, every single residential unit built between now and 2040 has to be close to or in a downtown or part of a new urbanism suburban location," says Nelson.

"Of course that won't happen," Nelson is quick to add. "We build 1.5 million to 2 million homes a year to keep up with market demand and to replace homes falling out of the market. By 2040 we will have 160 million new housing units, of which 30 percent, or 50 million homes, have to be built to meet the demand for new urbanism."

Resistance to developing in urban areas remains fairly strong because of higher costs. Yet, the result of such intransigence will be higher demand and that will drive up prices.

"At a time in our history when we need to build on average 1.5 million units a year to keep up with housing formation, no one has figured out how to build that much each year in infill development," avers John McIlwain, a senior fellow for housing at the Urban Land Institute. "With higher gas prices you will see demand growing faster than supply. Unfortunately, that will push moderate-income, middle-income, and younger people further out."

It's a devil's bargain: The housing further out will be less expensive, but transportation costs are growing.

"We are entering interesting times, not so much because of what is happening in the inner cities, but what is going to happen on the outer edges," says McIlwain. "What is going to happen to the value of homes in those newer developments where foreclosures are now going on. Will their value recover?"

McIlwain is not optimistic. "Those new developments on the outer edges of suburbia have been hit hard and are troubled. There are a lot of vacancies and growing crimes—all kinds of neighborhood deterioration. That takes a long time to turn around, and we do not have the tools for it, particularly at the outer edges."

Over the next decade, gasoline prices will continue to go up and down. As noted, at first people will make decisions concerning their vehicles, turning to smaller cars and hybrids. Eventually, a decision will have to be made about their house, too.

"Buying a new home closer to employment is not a snap decision," says Engelhardt. "I do not anticipate a near-term change in

location behavior—say, over the next two years. But, if I'm looking 5 to 10 years down the line, there will be locational changes.
Remember, typical homeowners stay in their homes about seven
years. Seven years from now, you will see the changes."

He adds, "Demand will shift as housing close to employment
will come at a premium. You will see prices in those areas rise as
prices in bedroom communities decline."

Here's one way potential homebuyers who want to live closer
to employment or infill areas can pay that premium: They will
fork out less money on automobiles. "In this country, 25 to 26 percent of household spending goes to the home and 19 percent to
transportation, mainly cars. Europeans spend 13 to 14 percent
on transportation. One hundred years ago, Americans only spent
3 percent on transportation," explains Leinberger. "The average
cost to own and operate a mid-sized vehicle is estimated to be about
$7,800 a year. If homeowners drop one car and use those dollars for
principal and interest on a 30-year mortgage, they can get $150,000
extra in a mortgage."

Local governments will be changing their perspectives on housing, because they need to. Already, says Nelson, suburban communities that have leaned heavily on single-family detached homes
are experiencing declining tax revenues and have to raise property
taxes to cover lost revenue. "One suburban county in Virginia has
seen a one-third decline in the value of homes in two years," says
Nelson. "They raised the property tax to keep revenues coming in
so they can pay police and teachers. It's happening in other suburban counties as well."

These counties shouldn't expect that time will heal these
wounds. "The dirty rotten secret is homeowners in these suburban
counties won't ever make money on their homes," Nelson says.

So, here is the consensus opinion among urban theorists: The
second decade of this century will bring wrenching changes to
the American landscape, and much of it won't bode well for those
developments planned and zoned on the fringes of metropolitan
areas.

"There will be a surplus of large-lot, single-family homes out
on the fringe that will become vacant, torn down, or occupied by
low-income families," says Leinberger. "Their value will be far below
replacement value. If it costs $100 a foot to build a single-family
home on the fringes, you won't be able to sell it for $100 a foot."

According to some estimates, of the 57 million large-lot, single-family homes in the country, some 22 million will have a hard time finding buyers in the years ahead.

"In essence, we are at the beginning of a structural change in the housing market," Leinberger concludes. "We are talking about a structural change where much of the product built on the fringes in the first decade of this century will have a hard time finding buyers. Obviously some home products will do well, but most homeowners will get clobbered."

Bonus Box

Affordable Housing

Back in 2002, when I first started writing about affordable housing, I was told that the country needed to build 100,000 affordable housing units a year just to maintain stability because about the same number of units bled out of the market every year due to obsolescence.

The trouble is, due to a combination of high development costs and the maintenance of lower than market rate rents, affordable housing doesn't actually pencil out. So to spur development, back in 1986, Congress, in an unusually wise move, created an incentive program called the Low Income Housing Tax Credit and it has been incredibly successful for over 20 years.

The program worked for a couple of reasons. First, the federal government awarded the tax credits to the states so they could allocate as needed. Second, beyond the tax credits themselves, affordable housing was still left up to private investment. The way it worked was very simple. Developers would bid for the right to receive tax credits, which were then resold (through syndicators) to investors, who could use the tax credits as a direct reduction in federal tax liability over a 10-year period. The proceeds from the sale of tax credits were used to help fund development.

This always seemed to be a very stable market, but like everything else in the world of real estate investment, things got a little out of whack during the first years of the twenty-first century, only to deflate after the subprime debacle of 2007.

Until then, major U.S. corporations—telecommunications, cosmetics, manufacturing, chemical—were all investors in tax credits. But as yields fell and a profound yearning by the GSEs (Fannie Mae and Freddie Mac) and banks for the credits increased, the corporations fell out.

"Early on you had a lot of manufacturing companies that realized a lot of taxable income and were interested in sheltering some of that through tax-advantaged investments so they were buying credits," explains Tom Booher, executive vice president at PNC Multifamily Capital. "As yields continued to fall to the point starting around 2006 that they were below 5 percent, those companies didn't see that to be an attractive enough yield to continue to invest. In return, there were a number of banks that had Community Reinvestment Act needs and could meet those by investing in tax credits so they entered the market."

The result was a lack of diversity, says Bob Moss, a senior vice president and director of origination for Boston Capital Corp., a Boston-based real estate investment company that creates funds to invest in low-income housing tax credits (LIHTCs). The market in recent years has been dominated by the GSEs and banks that were fulfilling their Community Reinvestment Act (CRA) requirements.

Unfortunately with the credit crunch and residential housing shakeout, the GSEs and the banks are no longer showing profits and the demand for tax credits has dried up very quickly.

However, in the good old days, back when the GSEs and banks were gobbling up LIHTCs as fast as deals appeared, the demand was so intense that prices were pushed up and yields down.

Generally, a dollar in tax credits sells for $0.80, but in the few years before the subprime crash of mid-year 2007, they were selling in the $0.90 range, very close to $1, says Andrew Weil, executive managing director of Centerline Capital Group, the New York-based subsidiary of Centerline Holding Co., an alternative asset manager focused on real estate funds and financing. In 2008, the tax credits were back selling at about $0.80 and into the $0.70 range.

"At 90 cents on the dollar there were a lot of dumb developers making money," says Moss. "Tax credits were oversubscribed and any deal, no matter the strength of the general partner or developer, would find an equity source and get syndicated."

Real estate developments take a long time to get done. Back in 2006 and 2007 many developers were planning on getting close to $1 for every tax credit allocated, but by 2008 when they were ready to begin construction they found out they were only getting $0.80

Continued

(Continued)

for allocated tax credits. As a result they could no longer make their projects pencil out.

"The existence of every new developer entity is going to be challenged," says Moss. "Those developer groups that have sufficient cash flow and lean and mean staffs will focus their attention primarily on their portfolio as opposed to new production."

As a result of all this turmoil, the affordable housing market looks bleaker than it has over the past 20 years. The big buyers of tax credits, the Fannies, Freddies, and Bank of Americas are losing money so they don't need tax credits. In fact Fannie and Freddie, which have since been taken over by the federal government, have losses so deep it will take a couple of years even under conservatorship to get out of the muck.

With less bidding on tax credits, developers have turned to individual municipalities to try to cobble deals together. Land and construction costs remain so high that developers cannot build housing, charge submarket rents, and make a profit without a local government helping to buy down the cost of land, offer tax breaks, or use their bonding authority to offer subsidies.

Centerline raises money and equity to invest in tax credit deals, explains Weil. "And from 2004 through 2007, we raised around $1 billion to $1.2 billion each year to invest in deals. We will be under $1 billion in 2008."

The affordable housing industry is an $8 billion industry, Weil adds. "That's the amount people would raise annually to invest in affordable housing. In 2008, projections are that the numbers might be down to $4 billion."

By 2008, several syndicators moved to the sidelines trying to figure out if this was a business in which they still wanted to devote a lot of resources.

PNC's Booher expected 2008 to be a good year for his company in terms of raising capital. "We will have close to a record year in 2008 in the amount of credits that we are purchasing and syndicating," he says. "But the number of doors we will actually finance will be off 5 to 10 percent. There are definitely a number of projects that are getting allocated and built. It's just not the same numbers that we have seen over the past couple of years."

When will the affordable housing market get back on solid ground again?

"By the end of this decade, we will have cycled through all this and returned to a healthy market," says Moss. That seems to be the consensus of opinion.

"Not until the next decade," echoes Michael Novogradac, a managing partner with Novogradac & Company LLP, a San Francisco-based CPA and consulting firm with a specialty in tax-credit-assisted multifamily and affordable housing. (What could change the time frame is a housing stimulus package being tossed around in Congress.)

"To get the affordable housing market stabilized, a couple of infra-structure issues should be settled," says Novogradac.

First, the state agencies need to get tough. They need to say to developers, "Look, if your project doesn't work, then give us back the credits." The state agencies can then reallocate the credits to another developer who can make an investment at a lower credit price. If you structured your deal in 2007 based on tax credits selling for $0.95 and you only get $0.75, your deal won't work. If you structured your deal today for $0.75 per tax credit, you can get something done.

Second, yields need to rise. "When tax credit prices reached $1 you had people investing at a 4.5 percent yield after tax," Novogradac says. "From a risk perspective that was way too low. The yield you got on tax credit investing was not much better long term than on a municipal bond, which presumably has AAA guarantees. There was no rhyme or reason why those investments should have been done."

Finally, investors need to differentiate. LIHTCs were selling like homogeneous hotcakes, but Novogradac stresses, they should sell with yields based on the risk factors of the individual property. Think of it this way: An affordable housing development in San Francisco and a comparable product in rural Indiana probably have a few different risk factors, to say the least.

PART

V

LEISURE REAL ESTATE

CHAPTER ELEVEN

THE MARKET FOR SECOND HOMES

Some lean years ahead; Expect an unprecedented worldwide boom in the next decade

T he street that I live on counts about 24 homes and quite frankly I don't know everyone who lives on my block. However, of those people I do know, I'm guessing about 10 percent of the families own second homes. If I spoke with the folks with which I have no more than a nodding acquaintance and learned if they had a place in the mountains, I estimate the number of second-home owners on my street could probably rise to 20 percent.

Taken by itself, my street would probably be considered a fairly mainstream middle-class neighborhood, although there is a higher than usual number of very successful small-business owners who live on the block.

My neighborhood in Mesa, Arizona, is somewhat reflective of other middle-class environs, which means if I extrapolate in a reasonable manner, I can conclude that the proportion of the U.S. population that owns second homes should be between 10 and 20 percent. As it turns out, that's about right. The National Association of Realtors reports 10 percent of U.S. homeowners also own a second home. Gary

Engelhardt, an economics professor at Syracuse University's Center for Policy Research, who undertook a study on housing trends among baby boomers puts the percentage at 15 percent.

My suppositions aren't always so correct. When I grew up in the suburbs, most families had just one automobile. Today, almost all nonurban families have at least two cars, maybe three. On my street, every family has two or three cars parked in the garage or on the street at any one time. That led me to think that if we've gone from being one-car families to being two- and three-car households, maybe we are also heading to a point where we will also become two-residence households.

Although there was a major jump in this direction in the last half of the twentieth century, the percentage of households that owns two homes hasn't changed much over the past two decades. Whether we use the 10 or 15 percent data point, percentage expansion hasn't increased although the numbers of second homes under ownership has significantly expanded over the same two decades.

As I was taught by those in the know, when it comes to second homes, it remains a sector that sails on demographic waves.

"All you see happening in the second-home market is driven by demographics," avers Engelhardt. "The peak years for owning second homes are from 50 to 65 years of age, with the true percentage peak coming during the late fifties. About 22 percent of people in the 55- to 59-year-old age bracket own second homes. Between 60 and 64, homeownership percentage drops into the 13 to 20 percent range. After 65, second-home ownership drops off dramatically."

As it so happens, the peak years for second-home ownership matches the maturation of the original baby boomers, which is why the boom in second homes is often solely laid to that particular group.

Boomers who were born between 1946 and 1964 definitely have the means. They are in their peak earning years and many are also equity-rich, with homes that have appreciated over time. Match that buying power with low interest rates, and they are in a prime position to buy a second or even a third home. In addition, they may be planning to retire in a few years and want to lock in escalating prices at low interest to buy a home that serves as a short-term vacation residence and a future retirement home.[1]

This is a fairly accurate description. My son's in-laws, who live in York, Pennsylvania, are about 60 years of age and recently bought a second home in Hilton Head, South Carolina. They are maintaining the two homes, but even my daughter-in-law foresees a time in the near future when her parents would sell the York residence and move full-time to South Carolina, where already a number of her parents' friends have second homes, also with thoughts of retiring to the warmer beach and golf environment.

"The baby boomers are richer, healthier, and somewhat more mobile than their predecessors," observes Nicolas Retsinas, the director of the Joint Center for Housing Studies at Harvard University. "In some ways, the sweet spot in the second-home market is people in their fifties with good jobs and accrued savings."

Another way of looking at the demographics is from Howard Nussbaum, president of the American Resort Development Association. "There are 78 million baby boomers in this country who are somewhere between the ages of the early 40s to early 60s and they have more leisure time and more affluence than their parents' generation. I jokingly say that my grandparents saw retirement as sitting on a porch in a rocking chair, but today's generation entering their senior citizen years are all about Viagra and Botox. They have a different view of retirement."

Where We Were

It's not only that the baby boom generation is wealthier and maybe healthier than prior generations of Americans, but they also benefited from important financial changes that didn't exist for prior generations.

First, the World War II generation and subsequently their children came of age after the introduction of conventional financing. Back in the 1930s and 1940s, it was possible to get a mortgage but generally it was 10 years with a 50 percent down payment. The conventional mortgage that we know today—30-year, fixed-rate, low down payment—started in the late 1940s. By the time the World War II generation began slipping into their senior years, many started purchasing second homes in places like Florida or Hawaii. Second homes became a middle-class phenomenon in the second half of the twentieth century.

Around 1997–1998, baby boomers got a boost that their parents didn't have: tax reform. That allowed homeowners, after they sold their primary residence, to exclude up to $500,000 in capital gains from taxation. That meant homeowners did not have to buy a more expensive property after the sale of the primary residence to avoid a hefty capital gains tax. Instead, that same homeowner could buy a smaller and less expensive primary residence and a second home (whether used as a vacation home or an investment vehicle) with the tax-free gain. Obviously, this made second-home buying more financially attractive than ever before.[2]

"In previous years there was a lot of prosperity, people had a lot of equity in their homes, lines of credit were fluid, and people's aspirational needs grew with their ability to financially afford things," notes Ed Kinney, vice president of corporate affairs for Marriott Vacation Club.

The tax reform at the end of the 1990s was very timely because it was closely followed by the Internet/technology bust, which collapsed the stock market. As a result, many homeowners began purchasing second homes to diversify their investments. Real estate gains offset stock market declines; from 2000 to 2004, existing home price appreciation increased 55 percent while the S&P 500 index declined 15 percent. The housing market presented an attractive alternative to stocks, so many investors not only traded up on their primary residence but also bought homes and condos in Florida, Nevada, Arizona, and Southern California. The national share of purchase loans for second homes increased from 8.6 to 14.2 percent during the 2000–2005 time period.[3]

"We saw a sustained increase in the second-home purchases following the tax law changes on capital gains," says Walter Molony, a senior associate with the National Association of Realtors. "We found a lot of people were using the equity from the sale of the former primary residence and trading down. Twenty-nine percent of buyers were using the capital from the sale of the primary residence to buy a second home; a huge number paid in cash. There were a lot of cash-out refinancings during the housing boom years."

When the single-family residence and investment property markets began to peter out in 2006, the market for vacation homes continued to be extremely active. The year 2006 turned out to be a peak year for vacation homes in terms of transactional activity with a record 1,067,000 homes sold, reports the National Association of Realtors. The median sales price for vacation homes in 2006 slid in at a comfortable $200,000, that was down from 2005, which sported record numbers: median sales price of $204,100.[4]

"In 2006, we saw a plummeting of investment sales (NAR separates second-home sales into vacation and investment properties), yet vacation homes rose to a record number of sales," says Molony. "In part, that was pent-up demand from people who had been trying to buy vacation homes during the boom but just couldn't find one in the area they wanted."

Where We Are Today

As I'm writing this chapter, I'm looking at the NAR's most recent report, which includes 2007. It is not a pretty read. To sum it up, 2007 was the year market factors finally caught up to the second (vacation) home market.

From 2003, the number of vacation home sales jumped from 849,000 to the record 1,067,000 in 2007. In 2004, the median price of a vacation home sat at $190,000, then stayed above $200,000 for the next two years. It was a solid run, but the market ran aground in 2007, with sales dropping 31 percent to 740,000, and the median price dropping severely to $195,000.[5]

One of the reasons for the decline in 2007 was that the speculators disappeared from the market, says Christine Karpinski, the director of Owner Community for HomeAway Inc. and author of *How to Rent Vacation Properties by Owner*. "Speculators were heavy into the market from 2004 to 2006, but in 2007 only 3 percent of the buyers were speculators."

Interest in second homes has been very high for a long time, but the difference in the years 2004 to 2007 was that it was achievable, says Karpinski.

In 2006, at the height of the second-home market, the NAR did a survey of second-home owners. This is what it found out.

- The typical vacation-home owner was 59 years old, had a yearly salary of $120,600, and purchased a property that was 220 miles from his or her primary residence.
- Eighty-three percent of second-home owners were married.
- The typical second-home owners spent 39 nights per year at their property. Seventy-five percent did not rent their vacation home.
- Seventy-five percent of vacation-home owners purchased for personal use; 33.3 percent purchased to diversify investments;

18 percent intended the home to become a primary residence in retirement.[6]

Has the interest in second homes diminished? Karpinski didn't think so, but she added it was very hard to read the market. "We are in a weird real estate time," she says. "People are nervous about investing in second homes, they are nervous about investing in the stock market, and they are nervous about the price of gas. People are paralyzed in regard to investments."

This fear of the market probably won't end anytime soon, Karpinski added, because the second-home market, like other real estate sectors, fell into a crisis of its own. There are a huge number of foreclosures on the market and although seemingly this would create bargains, the whole ugly environment makes many middle-class investors nervous. Until stability returns, Karpinski maintains the market will not come back too soon. "An NAR study said that 77 percent of the buyers they surveyed felt like this was a good time to buy a second home. But who did they interview? People who bought a second home last year," she says. "If people thought this was a good time to buy a second home, they would have bought one."

Where We Are Headed

Although Americans claim they buy second homes as part of a lifestyle decision, it is sometimes difficult to separate the personal use aspect from what is also an investment. As Harvard's Retsinas notes, this makes predicting the future of the market difficult.

"The demographic factors are very persuasive, but I do think to some extent the second-home decision is part investment and part function decision," he says. "In the short term, people will have second thoughts about the investment value of a second home and that will temper demand."

How long will demand be tempered? Well, that's the $64 million question. "People (nonprofessional investors) have very short investment memories," Retsinas says, "but in 2010, the memory of 2007 and 2008 will still be front and center. Whether it will still be front and center in 2015, who knows."

By the time the NAR did its second-home survey for 2007, the market had changed considerably. In listing the reasons for purchasing a vacation home, 84 percent of the buyers wanted to use the home for vacation; 30 percent to use as a primary residence in the future; 26 percent to diversify investments; and 25 percent to rent to others. Other statistics of note: The median household income of 2007 second-home buyers settled in at $99,100; the property purchased could be located a median distance of 287 miles from the buyer's primary residence; and the typical buyer averaged 46 years old.[7]

It's the last number that sends the demographic-based, second-home *cognoscente* into rapture. Remember, the peak second-home ownership years are 50 to 59, so in a sense there is a whole second wave of baby boomers that have yet to move through this primo acquisition period of time.

As of 2008, there were 7.5 million vacation homes in the United States, as compared to 39 million investment homes and 75.2 million owner-occupied homes. Investment and second-home buyers tend to be baby boomers, says Molony. That brings us to the crux of the sector. "We have a large number of people in their prime years for buying a second home. The long-term demand tends to be favorable," Molony adds.

Some quick numbers from the NAR: There are 38.7 million people in the 50–59 age group and 45.3 million people in the 40–49 age group. Right behind them is 40.9 million more in the 30–39 age group. "Those younger segments will be driving the market over the next decade," says Molony.

The oddity of the second-home market is that millions of new second homes were built over the past couple of decades, but that was not because the percentage of baby boomers owning second homes increased, but due to more baby boomers being in the peak buying years than ever before, say the demographic researchers. In other words, more people, not a higher percentage of owners.

To put it another way, according to demographic researchers, none of the following have affected the second-home market to any degree: the opening of vast new regions of second-home locales beyond Florida and California, such as North Carolina, Nevada, and Arizona; the movement of big residential developers into the second-home market; the vast amount of new marketing schemes; earlier boom period philosophy; increased wealth; or globalization. Only population expansion has had an influence on the second-home market.

"If you are thinking about the second-home market, this is about as good as it is going to get right now," says Engelhardt. "You've got the leading edge of the baby boomers right now around 60 years of age. Guys like Bill Clinton and George Bush. The leading edge of the baby boomers are in the peak second-home buying years. I am 42 years old, a baby buster. We are a smaller cohort."

He adds, "What's driving this market is not a greater percentage of people owning these homes, it is more people owning the homes."

In 2004, Engelhardt published a research paper titled "Study on Housing Trends among Baby Boomers," which partly addressed second-home ownership. Among the findings (most of which hold up today):

- In 2004, there were 43 million American households comprised of individuals aged 50 and older who owned their main residence, of which 15 percent, or 6.6 million households, also owned a second home.

- The typical second home is held for about 15 years, but turnover is higher; 45 percent of older homeowners with such homes disposed of them within a six-year window. Changes in marital status and health, not income or employment, drive the decision to dispose of a second home and, hence, prepay a second-home mortgage.

- Only 12 percent of owners intend to sell their main home and eventually occupy their second home.

- Despite anecdotal evidence, the rate of second-home ownership among 50- to 60-year-olds—the peak demanders for these properties among older households—has remained flat over the 12-year period from 1992 to 2004. The early baby boomers were no more likely to own such homes than older cohorts of homeowners.[8]

According to Engelhardt, it is very easy to predict the future of the second-home market because it's all demographics driven. Just based on population data, he predicts, the number of second homes will rise to 7.7 million in 2010 and 8.9 million in 2015. In 2004, when Engelhardt made those predictions he was forecasting that the second-home market would grow by 2 million in a decade. After 2015, the growth would be slower.

In 2007, there were 7.5 million second homes in the United States, reports the NAR. Engelhardt's predictions appeared to be holding up, but that was due to unforeseen circumstances. The years of 2004 through 2007 were peak years for second-home/vacation/investment properties, and the stock had been increasing about 12 percent a year, says Molony. On the investment side, sales of second homes were often more than double sales of vacation, or user-occupied, second homes. During the 2004–2005 years, sales of investment property second homes were over the 2 million a year mark. Even after that market collapsed, sales of investment second homes were relatively strong at 1.6 million in 2006 and 1.4 million in 2007.

Many of those investment second homes were in the same places that others bought vacation second homes: Florida, Arizona, Nevada, Southern California. The investment buyers have struggled. Some have walked away from their investments; others are holding on to real estate that is worth less than what they paid for it. In effect, the investment second-home market impinges the vacation second-home market. The median sale price of investment second-home properties peaked in 2005 at $183,500 and by 2007 dropped to a median sales price of $150,000. The numbers weren't in for 2008 as this book went to print, but the trend line of vacation-home and investment-home prices was still definitely going in the wrong direction.

Demographics aside, due to the credit crunch, economic uncertainty in some cases such as in South Florida, massive overbuilding, and a bust mentality, the second-home market will join the other real estate sectors as a part of the walking wounded at least until the start of the next decade.

Engelhardt tells me that his projections were done prior to the credit crunch, so they would have to be modified to take the economic slowdown into account, but he has yet to do a new study. "Think of my projections as a best-case scenario, but because of the credit crunch will end up far short," he says.

"The vacation-home market is trying to recover. I don't expect it to lose market share," Molony adds.

Here's what the experts and evidence are telling us in regard to second homes:

1. Based on American demographics alone, we have long-term prognostications that are extremely positive.
2. In the short term, at least until the start of the next decade, the second-home market faces innumerable problems, which

are symptomatic and systematic with most other real estate sectors.

There is one other theory going around that if it proves accurate will reinvigorate the second-home market. Let's call it globalization, and the author of this construct can be found in London. He's Liam Bailey, head of residential research at Knight Frank in Great Britain and author of a study called *The 2008 Annual Wealth Report.*[9]

In the report, Bailey wrote, "The boom in second-home ownership over the past decade will be as nothing compared with the growth we will see over the next decade."

I gave Bailey a call.

As in the United States, British and other western European baby boomers became enamored with second-home markets, which not only blossomed in places like Florida but also in Spain and other Mediterranean countries. And, as with the United States, this market is suffering from a credit crunch and weakened economies.

"There is a slowdown on the demand side, and it will be quite bad for at least two to three years," says Bailey. "You will see people losing money on second-home properties."

On the other hand, there will be an increasing supply of second homes as resort development amps up around the globe. "There will be a mismatch for a couple of years, but afterward the second-home market will recover with record price growth in the very best markets and a rapid take-up of supply," he adds.

In the second decade of this century, an unprecedented boom in second-home markets will arise chiefly for two reasons. First, prices will fall significantly over the next few years and then at some point values will start to look attractive, says Bailey. Second, and most important, the rising luxury and middle class in developing countries, from Eastern Europe to Asia, will be flooding into second-home markets worldwide.

"The ownership structures of second homes in the United States, United Kingdom, and European countries are fairly well established and mature, although there is room for more growth," says Bailey. "We are currently seeing a market slowdown and people unloading second homes. But in places such as Poland and Eastern Europe, not even mentioning Asia where there was no penetration of second-home ownership, primary home price inflation has been fairly healthy over the last five years."

Bailey gives this example: Many British citizens bought second homes in Bulgaria, where home prices were way below Western European equivalents. Now, the British are facing competition from local buyers who were not in the market even two years ago.

A tiny percentage of the Russian population have second homes, but the middle class is expanding and they will seek second homes elsewhere, whether it be Spain, Bulgaria, or the United States, says Bailey. And the same can be said for Brazilians, Chinese, and Indians.

"Rising affluence generates another market, second homes and holiday homes," says Bailey. "We have yet to see the full impact on demand for property from the rising mass affluent populations of Central and Eastern Europe, let alone from China, India, South Korea, and other Asian economies."

Bonus Box

Winter Resorts

As I have mentioned and as readers of my previous books know, I live in Mesa, Arizona, a suburban city of almost 500,000 people southeast of Phoenix. For about nine months of the year, the weather is great, but in the dead of the summer it's miserably uncomfortable. For folks who live in Arizona full-time, there are generally two thoughts about escaping the heat. The first is to go to the coast, in particular, San Diego, about a six-hour car ride, but just as popular is to have a vacation home in the mountains.

In Arizona, one of the most defined second-home markets in terms of attracting regional residents is the White Mountains. It's a shorter car ride than San Diego and at a 7,200-foot elevation, the weather is cool during the summer and skiing can be an option during the winter.

On my street, at least two families boast second homes in the White Mountains; another family has a place in Purgatory, Colorado. My street is probably not much different from a middle-class block of homes in Plano, Texas, or Marietta, Georgia. A certain percentage of residents have second homes in mountain areas of the country.

Since World War II, the migration patterns have been from the colder Midwest and Northeast to the warmer Sunbelt states. If you now live in a warm weather climate, why would you want a second home

Continued

(*Continued*)

at a beach? That probably was somewhat of a Pavlovian response when considering where to go for summer or winter vacations. That attitude is changing for altitude considerations, and I maintain more people are considering mountain resort locations.

For us heat denizens, mountain locales are multiseasonal getaways. In the summer, they are good places to flee the heat and since many mountain resort spots, at least in the West, are located near ski resorts, it's a place to go for winter sports. Indeed, multigenerations of families often meet at winter cabins for Christmas or New Year vacations. Another bonus for folks like me living in the Arizona desert or those on the Florida Gold Coast is a trip to the mountains to view the fall colors, which is always a terrific, short vacation.

Although there are grand second homes in places like Tahoe, Jackson Hole, Aspen, Crested Butte, Park City, and so on, for most people entering this market, the residence of choice is a condominium, mostly for convenience. Since a second home is only used occasionally during the year, maintenance is built in to the purchase price. You leave, lock the door, and when you come back a few months later, everything is as you left it. There's no worry about mowing the lawn, trimming back hedges, or even maintaining the hot tub. If there's a break-in, which is less likely because security is generally better, you are informed immediately.

The trend line for winter resort area condo sales has been moving upward, especially for the baby boomers: folks who are older, have money for a second home, and don't want to worry about maintenance.

In spring 2008, a National Association of Realtors study reported that while sales of vacation homes in 2007 fell 31 percent, sales of vacation condos barely slipped, down only 2.8 percent. The result is that condos garnered a subsequently larger share of the vacation-home market in 2007 and now controls 29 percent of the total sector. The NAR also noted, while the detached single-family home made up 80 percent of primary residences, it was only 59 percent of vacation homes; condos and townhomes accounted for 16 percent of primary residences and 36 percent of vacation properties.[10] Although all that looked good, the vacation condo market couldn't avoid getting hammered by the credit crisis, and median prices dropped 10 percent from first quarter 2007 to first quarter 2008.[11]

Well, not all vacation condo markets got beat up. High-end locations remained strong.

The folks at Slifer Smith & Frampton Real Estate in the Vail, Colorado, area sent me some amazing data: In 2003, the average condominium price in Eagle County (Vail, and so on) stood at $443,900; by the end of 2007, the average price had risen to $997,624.

Early in 2008, *Barron's* magazine looked at Vail Resorts Inc., the publicly traded company that owns and operates the resorts at Vail, Beaver Creek, Breckinridge, and Keystone in Colorado, and at Heavenly in California. The magazine liked what it saw. Baron Capital Management owns 12 percent of Vail Resorts and Ron Baron, a principal of the company, told *Barron's:* "Vail properties are selling for $2,000 a square-foot—it's getting to be like Dubai."[12]

Things aren't much different in Jackson Hole, where the median home price totals $1.9 million, and the median price of a condo stands about $900,000 to $1.1 million, says William Van Gelder, an associate broker with Sotheby's International Realty in Jackson Hole. "In 2007, condo prices rose 21 percent."

In 2008, Van Gelder predicted the overheated condo market would slow along with the economy, but condo prices would still be climbing, just along a single-digit, not double-digit, trajectory.

High-priced condo markets in winter resort areas aren't recession proof. After the dot-com blowup at the turn of the millennium, the rise in condo prices in both Vail and Jackson Hole stalled, even deflated. "Still, for people who live here, real estate prices didn't decline as much as their stock portfolios," says Van Gelder.

Luckily for the wealthier set, it takes longer for high-end home prices to recede. In Eagle County, the toughest year for condos arrived in 2003 (about two years after the dot-com and 9-11 recessions) when average sale prices dropped more than $200,000. For Vail and Jackson Hole, prices will probably weaken around 2009 or 2010.

My dream location for a vacation condominium is not the nearby White Mountains or even the western states of Colorado and Utah, but to have a place in Canada. So, I checked in with Pat Kelly, president of The Whistler Real Estate Company Ltd., a 30-year force in the Whistler, British Columbia, property market.

Whistler is a planned community that consists of 67 percent condos and townhouses and the remainder single-family residences. Kelly explains, "The average price of a condo has gone from $450,000 to $580,000 since 2001, although a small studio can still be found in the $250,000 range."

Unlike western ski locations in the United States, condo prices in Whistler haven't been on a steady rise. Even though 2007 was the area's second best year in terms of sales, the four prior years weren't very strong.

Continued

(Continued)

It's difficult to predict even the near future for Whistler as it, along with Vancouver, plays host to the Winter Olympics in 2010; the city is being repositioned as a four-season resort area (warm weather activity infrastructure being built up); and the Canadian and U.S. economies haven't been running on parallel courses for many years now.

"If you are an investor, I would expect prices in Whistler to be very safe," says Kelly, "with a trend line upward over time, simply based on supply and increasing demand."

What's important to note about mountain vacation spots is that when it comes to real estate investments they are in some ways similar to beach locales. There is very little raw land left for building, so there is a limitation as to how much new product can be constructed.

Most resorts—even those attached to ski mountains—are surrounded by national forests and parks, where there is no private development. In addition, strict environmental standards are usually adhered to in mountain communities to either protect the land itself, conserve water, limit damage to forest, or maintain a balance with local wildlife.

In Teton County, Wyoming (city of Jackson, Teton Village, and so on), only about 3 percent of the land is private and about half of that has been given over to conservation easements.

Also, unlike places such as the Gold Coast of Florida where high-rise condos dominate, you would almost never see such a structure in a mountain community. It would be considered a blight. In the Jackson Hole area, the highest building can only be 46 feet—four stories.

The old adage about investing in beachfront property—God only created so much of it and therefore beachfront would always be valuable—may not apply to mountain property, but human-made limitations there do sustain land values in a similar manner.

CHAPTER TWELVE

THE MARKET FOR VACATION PROPERTIES

Many new hybrid vacation-home schemes to choose from; You're buying moments in the sun, not making an investment

Along with the effervescence in second-home markets over the past decade came a secondary boom in what is loosely called the hybrid vacation-home market. Many of these programs such as timeshare (now called vacation ownership), have been around for many years, but others such as destination clubs are very new.

The overriding concept in hybrid vacation homes was to address one of the key issues concerning second homes: Most vacation homes sit vacant more weeks, if not months, of the year than they are in use.

If you view your purchase of a condo in Aspen or a cottage in Maine strictly as an investment decision, then the "use" aspect of the property is less of a concern. However, on a cost-effective basis, if that condo in Aspen is lived in just for a month in December, a month in July, and maybe a month in April, there are still ongoing costs even for the nine months the property sits idle. When the property appreciates 40 percent over two years during a boom period, those costs are considered just a nuisance, but hyperactive home markets come and go every 10 years or so. When markets quiet, those ongoing costs, from taxes and insurance to maintenance or condo fees, can be debilitating.

The other driver of hybrid vacation homes has been the buy-in cost factor of a second home. In many desired locations, either at the beach or on the side of a ski mountain, the cost to acquire a residence rose beyond what the middle class could afford, so the only way to get into those locations was to purchase a time slot as opposed to the real estate itself.

Having said this, a number of the newer hybrid vacation-home schemes were actually designed for, and marketed to, the luxury class.

In some regards, the hybrid vacation-home market has mimicked the second-home market. Until 2006, demand outstripped supply. "There was a fever pitch of activity because consumers thought they were going to miss out on the market," notes Ed Kinney, vice president of corporate affairs for Marriott Vacation Club International. "Now, it's kind of truing out, and the hybrid vacation-home market is more stabilized. People are no longer coming to the market as if there was a fear of loss."

One result is that there is much more inventory on the market. But an inventory of what?

Hybrid vacation homes can be broken down into four basic food groups:

- *Vacation club or timeshare.* The purchase is of weekly increments.
- *Fractional ownership.* A percentage share ownership of an accommodation. Limitations on use are based on percentage share. Mostly high-end properties.
- *Destination clubs.* One-time membership fee (plus annual dues) allows members to vacation at any of the club's residences around the world. Mostly high-end properties.
- *Condo hotel or condotel.* Condominium ownership within a hotel structure. When not in use, the unit can be rented to guests as a hotel room.

"When you talk about hybrids, this is a market that is still going strong," says Kinney. "The timeshare market is strong. Fractional ownership is a tiny sector, but it has a great amount of momentum. There is a lot of development happening."

Although the hybrid vacation-home market continues to evolve, these categories have become established. That is not the problem going forward. Timeshares have been around since the 1960s and have worked through growing pains, regulatory issues, and even fraud problems. Now it has an established place in the market and considerable bulk. As of 2007, 4.4 million households owned one or more U.S. timeshare weekly intervals, reports the American Resort Development Association.

The newer schemes all have developed growing pains and a lot of investors will lose their Hawaiian shirts, if not considerable capital, over the next few years as the real estate markets tremble and these schemes attract more legal and governmental attention. This is where I'm going to concentrate my attention.

One of the complaints about the timeshare industry during its first growth phase in the 1970s was the way the products were sometimes marketed as investments. This got a number of early developers in trouble. Eventually the industry learned its lessons and except for excitable marketing in certain overseas locations, the word *investment*, has been erased from the script. Some of the new schemes such as condo hotels didn't learn this lesson, and a wave of lawsuits will wash over many of these developments.

Obviously, the hybrid vacation-home market could never be considered an investment because there is no actual real estate involved. In a timeshare, the consumer buys a time allotment, not real estate. The same is true for the destination club, which is a lot like joining a country club, except the country club grounds are many places not just one. In any case, there is no real estate investment by the individual, only by the organization.

Fractional ownership, condo hotels, and another sector called resort villas straddle the line in regard to an actual acquisition of hard assets, but because the concept involves other moving parts they shouldn't be considered an investment.

Marriott, the hotel company, has been a pioneer in vacation clubs since 1984, and has since offered fractional ownership and even in some cases whole residence ownership opportunities at its resort locations (these are called Grand Residences by Marriott and not villas). In none of those hybrid and whole ownership vacation programs will Marriott personnel, including those involved with sales, ever utter the word *investment.* The word has been banished from the Marriott dictionary.

The one thing Marriott doesn't do is condo hotels. "We looked at it," says Kinney. "It's a different product from a corporate standpoint. The way they were originally presented was that they were an investment for people to buy, use, and get a return on investment based on hotel occupancy. We didn't pursue it as a business."

Unfortunately for investors, they didn't scrutinize the business plan of the condo hotel as closely as did Marriott.

The Condo Hotel

The condominium hotel, better known as condo hotel or condotel, is a hybrid vacation home that on face value works as a use-based product, similar to a timeshare or fractional, but was perceived by buyers as an investment—and there lies a very sorry tale.

During the period of condominium pandemonium that began around 2002 and lasted into 2006, one of the investment spillovers was a staid older product, the condo hotel, that received a new, frenetic lease on life. An investor would buy a condominium in a hotel building and then allow the hotel to use the unit for guests when the owner was not in residence. The implication (perhaps a verbal message from the very aggressive sales personnel) was that the buyer would recoup investment costs and fees through the daily rental of the condo unit by the hotel. Except in rare instances this was a proposition that was never going to happen.

In 2006, at the height of the game, Lodging Econometrics, the Portsmouth, New Hampshire, consultant for the global lodging industry, counted 32 projects with 4,831 condo units opened with another 27 projects and 5,025 units to open the next year.[1] By 2008, the *Wall Street Journal* was calling the condo hotel "one of the most dangerous investments of them all." The *Journal* reported, "Many buyers purchased the hotel rooms from developers hoping to get paid every time the room was rented. But condo hotels, which account for as much as 10 percent of all hotel rooms under construction, are coming back to haunt many of the people who bought the units, the developers that constructed the buildings, and the operators hired to run the hotels."[2]

There are so many problems with condo hotels, but the initial mistake made by investors is that they never bothered to research the history of these hybrid vacation properties.

Three decades ago, the condo hotel was a popular concept in Latin America, especially Brazil, but it didn't work and as Mark Lunt, a principal in Ernst & Young's Hospitality/Real Estate unit, told me, condo hotels drove the Brazilian lodging industry "into the ground." In the United States, condo hotels were very popular and successful as a downscale lodging product in ski areas. It looked like a small condo, with a kitchen area and one or two bedrooms. The lobby with a check-in station was minimal. There were no amenities.

As for the product being an investment, Lunt chuckles at the thought. The old condo hotels were famous for losing money. In the 1970s, people would buy condo-hotel units, which always lost money, but the owners didn't care because they could write off these passive losses against income. The 1986 Tax Act disallowed passive losses against active income and the condo-hotel scheme died out.

Starting around 2002, the concept came back in a big way as a luxury product, but not because it was structurally any better. The condo hotel was a great way to finance new construction. The condo hotel as reinvented in this century was simply a financing mechanism for hotel developers to get a deal done. It had nothing to do with creating a better product for the consumer.

"This was really a program for the developer," says Lunt.

Let's say, for example, a developer builds a hotel at a cost of $100,000 a unit. The developer owns it for 7 to 10 years, then sells it at a tidy profit. However, if the same developer decides to build his grand lodging facility as a condo hotel, he presells each unit for $150,000, in effect taking all the profits upfront that would have accumulated across the next 10 years.

Problem number one: Bad management.

"That's where the problems came in," says Lunt. "Although the developer made promises about management, there was little incentive for the developer to stick around when times got tough, so they found another management company to take it over and take the heat for all the problems coming down the pike, such as not enough guests to fill the hotel rooms and not high enough rates to cover expenses or provide any return to the condo-hotel investor."

Problem number two: How developers operate.

Robert Goldstein, president and chief executive officer of Hospitality Consultants, is even more damning. "Many of the condo hotels developed over the past four or five years were done without concern for the underlying economics of the deal. What I mean by that is the developers looked at condo hotels as a panacea to build a property, take the profits out upfront, and in some cases there was little regard as to what was going to happen after it was built."

That leads us to problem number three: How hotels operate.

Of the major real estate asset classes, hotels are the most complicated because there is a layer of operating business atop the real estate. It's a 24-hour business sensitive to geopolitical events in Europe or new competition across the street. Usually, it takes three to four years for a hotel ramp-up to stabilize and on top of that the rooms are often discounted.

"You have to scratch your head and wonder what really is in it for the buyer," says Jared Beck, an attorney with the Miami law firm of Beck & Lee, whose practice is being increasingly devoted to issues involving condominiums and now condo hotels. "Look at Las Vegas, for instance. Everyone knows the hotels make their money off the restaurants and gambling and don't make any money off room rates. Why would you consider this an investment proposition? If you understand the hotel business in Vegas, you understand the rooms are not where the money is made."

That leads us to problem number four: Securities law violations.

Beck has been seeing more condo-hotel lawsuits because they were often marketed in such a way as to qualify for securities under federal or state laws, but not registered as a securities offering, thus entitling buyers to a refund of their deposits. The three key issues of contention are whether the condo hotels were marketed as investments, if buyers were limited as to how many days they could actually live in the unit, and rental pooling.

A number of the major hotel brands entered the condo-hotel market, which at first was definitely a win-win for everyone. By licensing their name, the hotel companies made easy money, developers got premium dollars on their units being associated with top hotel names, and buyers felt they were getting professional management.

"Those premiums, which were as much as 50 percent above the nonbranded condo hotels, by 2008 had already slipped to 15 to 25 percent," says Lunt. In addition, the hotel brands had to tweak the concept, basically requiring that 50 percent of the rooms remain dedicated hotel rooms, which gave them more control over the property.

Finally, we are left with problem number five: Overbuilding.

This little niche was so hot in the mid-decade that a ton of money was thrown at condo-hotel developments. After the usual long gestation period of planning, financing, and meeting regulations, most of the projects didn't get under way until around 2008, right in the middle of the economic downturn.

In mid-year 2008, Lodging Econometrics counted 50 projects with 8,182 units under way, plus an astronomical 167 projects with 39,347 units in the pipeline, which Patrick Ford, president of Lodging Econometrics, expected to get completed. "This is the last wave," says Ford. After this, he predicts very little, if any, new condo-hotel construction to happen.

The question going forward is, will anything save the luxury condo-hotel concept? Maybe in the long term but a revival won't come about until the next decade when short-term investor memory loss kicks in. For the remainder of this first decade of the twenty-first century, the condo-hotel concept is as close to dead as it has ever been over the past 30 years. So many buyers have thrown in the towel on their condo-hotel investments that there probably is not a bank today that would make a loan to this sector.

"A few years ago, the banks thought, 'Okay, we are getting sophisticated buyers who are going to end up owning these condo-hotel units.' If not, we've got recourse on these loans," says Goldstein.

Unfortunately, it all turned bad rather quickly.

"Instead of looking at the validity of these projects, the underlying economics, they looked to the borrowers who were taking down these units," Goldstein adds. "As it turned out, these people couldn't make the mortgage payments on their houses, much less on condo-hotel units. The banks started getting these back through foreclosure so they stopped lending to that sector. The banks have put the kibosh on new condo hotels."

Asked if we will ever see a condo-hotel building boom again, Ford responded, "It depends on how old you are. I won't see it."

Destination Clubs

Launched in 1998, the destination club concept is not only the newest hybrid vacation-home concept, but according to Jamie Cheng, co-founder of a web site that follows this market, it is also the fastest-growing segment of the luxury travel market.

Cheng stressed the words *luxury travel*, which itself is just a small part of the overall vacation-home industry, and the destination club is just a niche product of that. As of 2008, the destination club industry could count fewer than 6,000 members, whereas the timeshare industry, with a 30-year head start boasted over 3 million American members. Nevertheless, the concept has gained traction and as more people at the high end of the vacation-home market take a look at the concept, membership could grow exponentially.

When I first started writing about destination clubs around 2004, the sector was called luxury club membership, and it really began to gain notoriety because AOL founder Steve Case had jumped into the industry, unveiling Exclusive Resorts. The concept was interesting. Back then I wrote this summary in *Barron's*, which still holds up: "This program is structured like a country club and it is just as expensive. Club members pay a deposit, usually six figures, and then an annual fee of roughly between $15,000 and $20,000. But, instead of belonging to a singular country club, luxury club membership allows the participants to use any one of a portfolio of multi-million dollar residences (average value of home is $2.5 million) around the country and increasingly around the world."[3]

According to Nick Copley, founder of The Sherpa Report, or www.sherpareport.com, a web site for this part of the industry, the annual dues for most of the clubs are now in the $15,000 to $30,000 range, whereas initial fees are on the $200,000 to $500,000 continuum. There are some clubs with lower dues and fees and a couple with higher.

Copley also informs me that Exclusive Resorts now owns over $1 billion in real estate and several others own millions of dollars of real estate, which by the way has nothing to do with anyone who is a member. Although some destination clubs are trying to work a bit of equity participation into the membership, like a timeshare, the entry fees and dues only buy a member time, not property.

Remember, destination clubs are in the luxury tier of the hybrid vacation market, and as Copley points out, even with the high entry fees, on a cost per night basis the destination club is not out of line with accommodations for a large wealthy family that would seek something to rent with three to five bedrooms. The bulk of destination clubs average $1,000 to $2,100 on a cost per night basis.

Okay, I get that, but here's what bothers me about destination clubs. It's a time-use concept such as a timeshare or fractional, but someone must make money on the real estate. That someone is the managing company, which is harvesting your luxury travel dollars to pay for its investments in high-end real estate. Ten years from now, all that property could be worth infinitely more than it is today, making the principals in the management companies (not the members) wealthier than they are today. Steve Case probably doesn't need a few extra million dollars, but as a shrewd businessperson, he knows a good business plan when he sees it.

Even Copley concedes, "This has primarily been a real estate play."

In this young vacation sector, there has already been one major default, borderline scandal, and part of it had to do with the underlying real estate.

The industry is said to have been founded when Rob McGrath opened the destination club called Private Retreats in 1998. That company later became a joint venture under the auspices of Abercrombie & Kent. The whole thing later changed its name to Tanner and Haley. None of the permutations seemed to have helped as Tanner and Haley filed for bankruptcy in 2006 thus giving the nascent industry an early black eye.[4]

Supposedly, destination clubs own their own real estate, but something unusual went on behind the scenes at Tanner and Haley. In the bankruptcy filing, it was revealed that the "club only owned 67 homes instead of the 200 mentioned in its portfolio. Costly leases combined with under-priced charter memberships were key factors driving the firm's $64 million loss in 2005."[5]

The biggest losers in the bankruptcy were the members. "They lost their money," says Copley. "Some were putting over a million dollars into the club and they lost it." On paper anyway. Ultimate Resorts bought the assets of Tanner and Haley, and most of the members ended up with the new company.

The key question for consumers is, "Does the destination club of choice have the capital and assets available, if needed?" says Cheng. "We warrant there is always a rule that a number of members have to come in before the club can go out and invest. And you have to make sure the club is adequately capitalized, that the assets and capital cover member deposit liability."

What happened with Tanner and Haley? Cheng explains: "They were taking in capital and rather than putting it into homes and acquiring real estate, they were leasing a lot of the properties.

Without underlying real estate, the consumer had nothing to fall back on when things started to tumble out of control. To this day it is unclear where all the cash went."

One result of the Tanner and Haley mess was the creation of a Destination Club Association, which has put in place a number of best practices recommendations.

Also, it became apparent that while Destination Clubs looked like an easy business model, it was actually very complicated. "Back in 2005, a lot of investors, real estate developers, and businesspeople were teaming up, thinking this looked like the next big vacation-home trend. Let's get started acquiring homes and building up a membership," says Cheng. "So, they went off and got the first 20 to 30 members and the first 5 to 10 homes, and then they realized it got harder and harder as they tried to get bigger and bigger."

In scale, it becomes difficult to run a Destination Club. Not only do you have to market and acquire members, but you have to deliver the hospitality level you promised. Basically, you are operating 25 homes in 25 locations and each one needs a cleaning team—landscaping, housekeeping, maintenance—a lot different than 200 rooms in one hotel building.

In 2007, Copley counted over 20 different destination clubs of one sort or another, but the bulk of membership was just in a handful. Going forward, most of these smaller clubs will either fade away or merge into the bigger clubs, resulting in a niche industry with 5 to 10 players.

Both Cheng and Copley have run studies showing the concept is cost effective for those who need a large amount of rooms when they travel, which is probably one reason why the idea has caught on.

By the middle of the next decade, Cheng seems to think destination club membership will zoom up to a minimum 50,000-member households. If membership gets anywhere near that number, the hospitality giants, such as Marriott, will start picking off the bigger players. That would be a good thing, because it would stabilize this nascent industry, which today still has an aura of the Wild West about it.

Fractionals

Although the concept of fractional ownership is not new, this hybrid vacation-home product really took off in the first decade of the twenty-first century, partly driven by new development and partly driven by the influx of major hotel companies that moved into this sector.

Like timeshares, fractionals are a use-product, but unlike the timeshares, it is an investment in actual real estate because a fractional is deeded property. Also, fractionals are considered a product for the luxury set. However, there is a category like fractional but even higher-end, and it's called private residence clubs. In a sense, comparing a timeshare to a fractional or private residence club is like comparing a Hyundai to a Bentley.

"Private residence clubs are really designed for the very affluent market," notes Howard Nussbaum, president of the American Resort Development Association. "It's for the few percent of households that own a principal home, vacation home, maybe even a second vacation home, and are not interested in owning more stuff. They are interested in a very high-end experience with lots of services and surrounded by people like themselves. They can buy six weeks' use at a Ritz Carlton or St. Regis and have a better vacationing experience with the extended family."

With fractionals and private residence clubs, investors own a percentage share of the asset, usually on a longer timescale than a timeshare—as small as 1/8th to 1/12th of a year. So at minimum, a fractional owner has one month of the year at a particular location.

"The big thing is matching your usage to your ownership, so if you look at how people use their vacation homes, most occupy them 25 to 35 days a year," says Copley. "By buying into a fractional you are buying four to eight weeks of ownership a year and paying only for the amount of time at the real estate that you are realistically going to use."

On the downside, everyone's ownership has to be balanced in terms of best times of year. If your fractional is at a ski resort, not everyone is going to get the best weeks of winter. There are compromises.

Despite fractionals being a deeded hybrid vacation home, beware of any pitches calling this a real estate investment with great potential for appreciation. Any type of investment with such a complicated ownership structure is not going to reward investors much in the way of an interesting return. It's best just to think of it as a lifestyle choice, because they are not cheap to buy into.

"Developers indicate fractionals are generating price premiums of 100 to 200 percent per square foot over full-ownership products, although with higher marketing cost and longer absorption periods," Mark Lunt, a principal in Ernst & Young's Hospitality/Real Estate unit, writes in his company's "Hospitality Top Ten Thoughts for 2008."[6]

Lunt also observes fractionals fare better when developed alongside established hotels, as the hotels may encourage potential buyers as well as critical mass for the development.

The growth of fractionals has been so strong that the market continued to expand even through the subprime mortgage crisis year of 2007.

"Fractionals have garnered less interest from speculators and, as a result, are weathering a declining real estate market better than condominium hotels," Lunt says.

Major hotel companies from Marriott to Starwood to Fairmont like the fractionals concept, so expect considerable expansion of this product well into the next decade.

Bonus Box

Resort Villas

As I was organizing this chapter, I received an e-mail from an old friend who works at a public relations agency in New York. The agency specializes in the travel industry, and the e-mail concerned two new accounts. Oddly, both were about a vacation-home category that I refer to as resort villas, although they go by other names. Marriott, for example, calls its resort villa product Grand Residences.

Resort villas are whole ownership homes located on the grounds of a resort and maintained and serviced by the resort for annual built-in fees over and above the acquisition price. Often they are rented, but they don't have to be.

The properties my friend marketed were unusual. The first was called African Homesteads and essentially consisted of private homes in the Phinda Game Reserve in South Africa. Her comment to me was "For $6 million, a second-home buyer could own a piece of an African game reserve complete with private cook, housekeeper, butler and ranger, tracker, and vehicle."

The second property was also foreign, but a little closer to what we would expect in a resort villa. It was located on the grounds of the Amanyara Resort on the island of Providenciales in the Turks and Caicos Islands. Prices here ranged from $10 million to $20 million for a villa. Her comment: "Here the jet set (where most of the clientele actually do own their own jets) can enjoy the exclusive service for which Amanyara is renowned."

I decided to call Michel Neutelings, chief operating officer of Amanyara, and I happened to get him as he was wandering around the streets of New York.

"Well, how are the villas doing?" I asked.

"Fabulously. We just closed on another one last week," Neutelings responded. Of the 33 villas on the Amanyara property, 28 have been sold, the majority to Americans but also some to Canadians and Europeans. Not bad considering Amanyara does no true advertising of the properties and uses no real estate agents. It's all word of mouth.

"With the economic crisis in the United States, isn't this a bad time to be selling villas?" I continued.

"Because our real estate is at very high price points, the people who buy these aren't affected by the credit crisis," he said. "Many pay with cash. This is a rarified air market."

He added, "There was a huge demand for a high-quality product of this type. The Caribbean used to be for honeymooners; now families come down and might need three or four rooms in a hotel or have to rent a house."

Obviously, the solution was to acquire your own house. And if you wanted a luxury property on some "hot" Caribbean island such as Anguilla, Turks, or St. Barts that is not part of a resort, you can find one but then you have to search out your own maintenance, maid, and security services. On the other hand, a resort villa will be taken care of, all the time. No headaches.

When I received the e-mail from my friend mentioning the two villa properties, it got me thinking that there might be an emerging trend here and I should include something on the subject in this book. So I then checked in with Alfredo Merat, founder of the Villas of the World web site, to see what was going on in this market.

"In all fairness, this is a niche market," says Merat, "but it is a trend and it has been growing." Well, it had been growing until 2008.

"In 2006 and 2007, a lot of wealthy buyers loved the idea of acquiring, thinking if they stay at a resort for three to four weeks why not buy a villa," Merat said, "but in 2008 we started to see a lot more rentals as people were shying away from buying."

Continued

(Continued)

What happened in the resort villa market, says Merat, is that the middle market has disappeared, but the high end is still doing well.

On the www.villasoftheworld.com web site, there are few homes for sale, but an increasing number of desperate rentals.

That got me thinking. If you're going to spend $10 million for a resort villa, do you really want to rent it out? Merat laughs. "I have this property listed on our web site that is seven bedrooms, seven bathrooms, private tennis court, and on the beach. It fetches $1.9 million in rental income yearly."

Over at the Amanyara villas, Neutelings says that at first there were some owners who didn't put their villas into the rental pool, but the fees for maintenance, insurance, utilities, and so on, run to $150,000 a year and the rental program seems to cover that. Now all owners are in the rental pool.

Down in the Caribbean, Neutelings is keeping a wary eye on the resort villa market, which has slowly been growing. He figures the Caribbean could handle another three or four resorts at the very high end, especially in places like the Turks, St. Barts, Anguilla, or Nevis. However, there's talk of 15 new projects, which Neutelings doesn't think the market could handle.

Merat's web site is mostly concerned with rentals, and he doesn't separate the resort villa market from general vacation-home rentals. What he sees is not pretty. The general economic slowdown has absolutely crushed this market. As an investor, if you bought a vacation property thinking you would make back some capital on rentals, it is just not going to happen—at least not for a long time.

Merat predicts this market won't come back until sometime early in the next decade.

Timeshares

Since this chapter is about hybrid vacation-home markets, I would be remiss if I didn't mention the oldest and largest segment of this market—timeshare, or as it is known today, vacation club.

Although I'm not a fan of the concept, it is not only hugely successful but so far has managed to expand even against the strong headwinds of a deep economic malaise in this country.

The thing to remember about timeshares is that it is not in any way a real estate investment. In fact, it probably shouldn't even be considered an investment. With a timeshare, you buy "use," generally two weeks at a single resort. That was the original sell. However, what really has made timeshares extremely viable and where I think the attraction resides is that owners of a particular time slot can exchange their two weeks for another two weeks at another resort somewhere else in the world. There are numerous exchanges to do that.

A friend of mine who many years ago bought a timeshare, for a period of time was transferred by his employer to The Netherlands. He barely took advantage of his timeshare while he lived in the States, but in Europe he was able to exchange his slots at a U.S. resort for a timeshare slot some place on the European continent and this became his vacation for all the years he was there.

"People who buy vacation ownership do not do so for investment quality; they buy them for the value proposition in terms of use," says Howard Nussbaum, president of the American Resort Development Association (ARDA). "They buy them for better vacationing and because there are fewer costs and responsibilities than owning a second home. We call this a lifestyle investment, not a financial investment."

Vacation ownership is very compelling on an expenditure level, Nussbaum adds. "You can spend $20,000 and own a two-bedroom condo for a week every year and you can pass that on to your kids. It might cost you $5,000 to maintain it, but that would not cover the closing costs on some second-home developments. The question is, do you want to own an asset that is available to you 365 days a year or do you want a vacation apartment that is available to you when you want a vacation?"

Marriott International Inc. was the first "branded" hospitality company to enter the timeshare industry back in 1984. The Walt Disney Company, another major timeshare resort owner, didn't come into the market until the mid-1990s.

"At the end of 2006, it was our eleventh consecutive year of over 20 percent average annual growth in our timeshare sector," says Ed Kinney, vice president of corporate affairs for Marriott Vacation Club International, the company's half-billion-dollar vacation club subsidiary. "In 2007, growth tapered off to the high teens."

"That slowing was not due to the subprime mortgage blowout in the summer of that year and the subsequent credit crisis," says Kinney, "but the result of not being able to build new properties as land costs had become so high during the prior years when real estate markets were booming."

As I write this chapter, the last complete studies on the timeshare market by ARDA was as of January 1, 2007, when there were 4.4 million

Continued

(Continued)

households that owned U.S. timeshare weekly intervals, a 7 percent increase over the year before. Total sales for 2006 had reached $10 billion, up 16 percent from the year before; 2007 numbers were up 6 percent over 2006.

Nussbaum predicted his industry would fare well over any economic downturn. As a use product and not a financial investment, "It is less susceptible to the peaks and valleys of the economy."

Nussbaum was wrong. Early in October 2008, Marriott reported third quarter earnings that were less than stellar, with a 28 percent decline in profits. According to the firm, lodging operations held up "admirably" during the downturn, but the company sustained big hits to its timeshare business, "which was significantly impacted by the financial markets."[7]

For the long term, Kinney strongly suggests Marriott's business will start picking up again heading into the next decade and that's simply because of economics and not the economy. Raw land prices are coming down, which makes new development "doable" again, he says. The company has been active, opening new vacation club properties overseas, in the Caribbean and select U.S. locations; that activity level is expected to increase with an increase in new U.S. development.

Afterword

I began writing this book in the winter of 2008 and finished the last chapter just about the first of August that same year.

However, 2008 was a tumultuous year and I remember as I was writing the book that it was difficult to stay ahead of the news. Eventually, events did get ahead of me because by late summer and early autumn, the financial world shifted; Fannie Mae and Freddie Mac were taken over by the federal government; Merrill Lynch, Washington Mutual, and Wachovia were sold; Lehman Brothers went under; and AIG needed federal intervention.

Fortunately, I got the manuscript back around the first of October to do some editing, and I was able to update the book where it was relevant. I have to admit I was a little nervous because, although I was, in some regards, predicting where markets will be in the near- to mid-term future, I was wondering if the calamities of third quarter 2008 would alter the courses of the particular asset classes about which I was writing.

Much to my relief, the corporate changes among the financial institutions didn't change my assertions. The reason for that was I mostly focused on market fundamentals and trend line progressions. There is the possibility that the vast new financial landscape could slow down the trend lines and postpone the recovery of individual markets. On the other hand, the changes could actually speed up recovery because the new institutions that control real estate would more likely move the bad stuff off their books, albeit at a very big discount. Once the market knows the value of all that real estate, the next group of investors can quickly strike their deals.

In the end, the players may change, but the real estate doesn't.

If all this drama feels déjà vu, well, that's because it is. Where we are today is largely a result of what happened with the financial markets 20 years ago: market turmoil, a huge swath of financial institutions failing, real estate repriced at vastly lower values, and new ownership emerging.

Does any of this sound familiar? The easing of federal regulations allows an existing financial sector to expand its involvement in real estate markets. The existing sector grows quickly and feverishly in the new playing field, and it appears deregulation has again been successful. In fact, deregulation did nothing more than increase the real estate gamble. Billions went into property investments only to have the markets fall apart in a cataclysmic crash. The new players disappeared from the playing fields and another virginal financial sector moved in, because finance, as with nature, abhors a vacuum.

In the 1980s, savings and loans, an industry that traditionally financed residential housing was allowed to cross over into financing commercial real estate. This led to a boom in everything from shopping centers and apartments to hotels and office buildings. In fact, every sector quickly became overbuilt and beginning in about 1987 real estate markets began to crash.

By the early 1990s, most of the thrift industry had disappeared and the real estate once owned and financed by that part of the financial world was taken over by the federal government, repackaged into mortgage-backed securities, and resold. The investment banking world realized there were huge profits to be made in mortgage securitization and from a tangential position in real estate financing, investment bankers became the engine of growth.

That is, until 2007, when the real estate markets began crashing anew. And like the S&L industry two decades before, the independent investment banking world, scorched beyond recognition by bad real estate investments, has all but disappeared.

The big question is, which new players will be able to take advantage of a massive redistribution of real estate ownership that is coming in the years ahead?

One of the important points I tried to raise in *After the Fall* is that many years pass between when real estate markets begin to crash until the time when some degree of stability, consistency, and appreciation is again reached. I personally subscribe to the minimum six-year rule: three years of decline and three years of rebalancing. Some, but not all, property markets began to fall apart in 2006. By 2007, residential real estate dropped into crisis mode; in 2008, the contagion spread to all real estate markets and financial institutions start to fall. The expectations are that 2009 will be the trough year, at least in regard to residential housing. According to the six-year rule, it will be the next decade before recovery begins.

Beyond just market plays, real estate has been undergoing significant structural changes, which I've tried to address as well. Obviously, trend lines and market fundamentals criss-cross, so one affects the other.

In *After the Fall*, I tried to look at the most important asset classes and cross-current trend lines. For the handicapper, here's a brief summary:

- *Office.* This is the one sector that may change beyond what I previously reported, mostly because of the consolidation in the financial services industry. Clearly, cities such as New York will be hit with an increasing amount of space dumped into the market. However, the important notion to take away is that New York and other major development-challenged cities remain the most attractive to institutional investors. Even with serious weakness ahead, investors would rather be in New York than in, for example, Indianapolis or St. Louis. Second-tier cities face bigger problems because of a smaller flow of investment dollars.
- *Industrial.* The fundamentals of industrial real estate don't vary much, so I focused on the product itself, which was shifting more to larger and larger distribution buildings as a result of supply chain globalization and consolidation of domestic distribution. That being said, a weakening consumer market adversely affects the demand for distribution and warehouse space.
- *Retail.* This sector is under assault due to a number of factors, the principal one being a consumer spending collapse in the face of a pre-recession economy. The pace of store closings picked up in 2008, a phenomenon accelerated by venerable store and restaurant chains going out of business. The second problem plaguing retail is that a lot of new product was built in coordination with new residential developments. When the housing market imploded and those new developments were never built out, those shopping centers became ghost towns.

- *Multifamily.* Unlike in the last major real estate recession at the end of the 1980s and in the early 1990s, most markets weren't overbuilt with apartments. An expected pickup in occupancy due to the fallout from the single-family housing market didn't materialize. With new development way down, the demand for rental housing will pick up steam in the next decade.
- *Green Buildings.* Not just about design and not just about saving the environment. Institutional investors want LEED-standard buildings, so those structures that are Green have a value-added factor.
- *Distressed Real Estate.* A couple of weeks before I began writing this Afterword, I attended a distressed real estate symposium in Chicago. Most of the attendees were investors, or potential investors as few were active. Months before when I had written this chapter, investors were waiting for property pricing to become more realistic. In some ways, it was comforting to know my chapter's main thesis had held: Buyers and sellers were still too far apart for widespread dealmaking.
- *Single-Family Homes.* Most everyone I spoke with on this subject believed the bottom of the market would be reached in 2009 when on a national level the value of residential real estate would stop falling. Even if correct, it won't be a time of celebration, because appreciation will be hard fought for years to come.
- *Condominiums.* Truly, some second-home, retirement-home condo markets such as Florida and, perhaps, Las Vegas are so overbuilt and so busted, it will take a decade to see improvement. In contrast, the population in cities will become denser in the future so the urban condominium has a stalwart future.
- *Insurance and Taxes.* The steep rise in home insurance costs are not evenly spread throughout the country. If you live away from the coasts and away from earthquake-prone landscapes, home insurance costs are barely a concern. Similar widespread discrepancies occur in regard to taxes, but the good news or bad news depends on local concerns.
- *Urban and Suburban Infill.* In 2008, the cost of gasoline rose to stratospheric levels, at least in regard to historical pricing. Eventually, the cost of commutation will be a concern for

individuals looking to buy a house and for industries seeking employees. Bad news for those unfinished developments in the far exurbs.

- *Second Homes.* The weakness in the second-home regions follows hard on the pace of primary residential markets. The good news for existing owners is second-home markets near beaches or in mountains are usually in places where growth is limited. Demand for second homes will regain strength in the next decade.
- *Vacation Homes.* Many new vacation-home programs—condo hotels, fractionals, and so on—were heavily promoted over the past two decades. As with the traditional timeshare, one is really just buying vacation time and not investing in real estate.

These are succinct summations of where I believe some of the main asset classes and real estate trend lines are headed. When I was writing the book in the early months of 2008, I was worried that I was being too pessimistic. Now, as I'm scribbling this Afterword during the first week in October 2008, a $700 billion bail-out bill has been passed by Congress and signed by President Bush. Yet, the stock market continues to nosedive. I'm actually wondering now if I've been too Pollyannish.

Notes

Chapter One: The Office Market

1. Maura Webber Sadovi, "Office-Market Downturn Weighs on Region," *Wall Street Journal*, February 6, 2008.
2. Ibid.
3. Steve Bergsman, "Buyers, Beware," *Barron's*, October 10, 2005.
4. Ibid.
5. Terry Pristin, "Financial Ground Has Shifted under a Record Deal, *New York Times*, November 7, 2007.
6. Antony Currie and Lauren Silva, "Why Dimon in the Rough?," *Wall Street Journal*, January 17, 2008.
7. Terry Pristin, "Financial Ground Has Shifted under a Record Deal, *New York Times*, November 7, 2007.
8. Steve Bergsman, "Buyers, Beware," *Barron's*, October 10, 2005.
9. Jennifer Forsyth, "Mr. Macklowe's $3 Billion Life Raft?" *Wall Street Journal*, February 20, 2008.
10. Ibid.
11. Jennifer Forsyth, "Zuckerman Takes Manhattan," *Wall Street Journal*, June 11, 2008.
12. Amanda Marsh, "Office Condos Weather Credit Crunch," *Commercial Property News*, March 1, 2008.
13. Susan Stabley, "Some Projects Leave Office Condo Market," *South Florida Business Journal*, March 2, 2008.

Chapter Two: The Industrial Market

1. Steve Bergsman, "Shocks to the Supply Chain," *Chief Executive*, April/May 2008.
2. ProLogis Forms New North American Property Fund to Acquire $1.8 Billion Industrial Portfolio from Dermody Properties/CalSTERS JV, www.prologis .com, July 12, 2007.
3. Maureen Webber Sadovi, "Developers Betting on Texas-Size Warehouses," *Wall Street Journal*, February 13, 2008.
4. Steve Bergsman, "Double-Barreled BOOM in Kansas City," *National Real Estate Investor*, June 1, 2008.

5. "ProLogis Releases New Research Reports on Industrial Property Markets and U.S. Construction Pipeline," www.prologis.com, March 31, 2008.
6. Ibid.
7. Chris Hawley, "Aerospace Industry Migrating to Mexico," *Arizona Republic*, April 2, 2008.
8. Ibid.
9. Jobwerx. "Two New Polymers Manufacturing Plants," www.jobwerx.com, October 18, 2007.
10. Economic Policy Institute. "States Continue to Hemorrhage Manufacturing Jobs," www.epi.org, December 12, 2007.
11. Chris Hawley, "Aerospace Industry Migrating to Mexico," *Arizona Republic*, April 2, 2008.
12. Steve Bergsman, *Maverick Real Estate Financing: The Art of Raising Capital and Owning Properties like Ross, Sanders, and Carey* (New York: John Wiley & Sons Inc., 2006).

Chapter Three: The Retail Real Estate

1. Elaine Misonzhnik, "Centro Nabs New Plan for $6.2B," *National Real Estate Investor*, February 28, 2007.
2. "2007 Year in Review," *Retail Capital Trends Monthly*, January 2008.
3. Lingling Wei and Randall Smith, "Wall Street Gears for Its New Pain," *Wall Street Journal*, March 3, 2008.
4. Kris Hudson, "The Democrats Are Coming, But Is That Enough," *Wall Street Journal*, April 2, 2008.
5. Kris Hudson and Jeffrey McCracken, "Retailers' Woes Weigh on Mall Owners," March 9, 2008.
6. "2007 Year in Review," *Retail Capital Trends Monthly*, January 2008.
7. Lingling Wei and Randall Smith, "Wall Street Gears for Its New Pain," *Wall Street Journal*, March 3, 2008.
8. Kris Hudson and Jeffrey McCracken, "Retailers' Woes Weigh on Mall Owners," March 9, 2008.
9. Ibid.

Chapter Four: The Multifamily Market

1. Alex Frangos and Michael Corkery, "Lehman's Property Bets Are Coming Back to Bite," *Wall Street Journal*, June 10, 2008.
2. Susanne Craig, "Lehman Wants to Short-Circuit Short Sellers," *Wall Street Journal*, April 1, 2008.
3. Alex Frangos and Michael Corkery, "Lehman's Property Bets Are Coming Back to Bite," *Wall Street Journal*, June 10, 2008.
4. Gleb Nechayev, "A Tale of Two Rental Markets," www.twr.com, March 21, 2008.
5. Alex Frangos and Michael Corkery, "Lehman's Property Bets Are Coming Back to Bite," *Wall Street Journal*, June 10, 2008.

6. "Market Trends," www.nmhc.org, May 2008.
7. Nick Timiraos, "Regional Buyers Go Apartment Hunting," *Wall Street Journal*, May 28, 2008.

Chapter Five: Sustainability

1. Transwestern: The Performance Edge in Real Estate. "What Is a Green Building," www.transwestern.net.
2. David Carini, "Building Green in SF," *San Francisco Bay Guardian*, February 27, 2008.
3. James Quirk, "Leading the Way for Green Design," *The (North Jersey) Record*, February 21, 2008.
4. Randyl Drummer, "REITs Buying into 'Green Premium,'" www.costar.com, October 17, 2007.
5. Daniel Taub, "U.S. Office Buildings Rated Energy Efficient Draw Higher Returns," www.Bloomberg.net, June 6, 2008.
6. Randyl Drummer, "REITs Buying into 'Green Premium,'" www.costar.com, October 17, 2007.
7. Brian Moynihan, "The Business of Climate Change: A New Leadership Opportunity," www.bankofamerica.com, October 18, 2007.
8. Mychele Lord, "Show Me the Money: Investment Real Estate Goes Green," *Buildings Magazine*, December 2007.
9. Ibid.

Chapter Six: Market for Distressed Real Estate and Loans

1. Susanne Craig and Randall Smith, "Merrill Aims to Raise Billions More," *Wall Street Journal*, July 29, 2008.
2. Robin Sidel, David Enrich, and Jonathan Karp, "Bank Fears Spread after Seizure of IndyMac," *Wall Street Journal*, July 14, 2008.
3. Mark Gongloff, "Room at the Inn: Oversupply Hits Hotels," *Wall Street Journal*, July 10, 2008.

Chapter Seven: The Single-Family Housing Market

1. Mark Gongloff, "Ahead of the Tape: Struggling to Fill Vacant Homes," *Wall Street Journal*, July 24, 2008.
2. Walter Molony, "Existing-Home Sales Down in June," www.realtor.org, July 24, 2008.
3. J. W. Elphinstone, "US Foreclosure Filings More Than Double," www.yahoo.com, July 25, 2008.
4. E. S. Browning, "Banks Rally, but Demons Still in Vault," *Wall Street Journal*, July 28, 2008.
5. J. W. Elphinstone, "S&P: Home Prices Drop by Record 15.8 Pct. in May," www.yahoo.news, July 29, 2008.
6. James Hagerty, "Number of Foreclosed Homes Keeps Rising," *Wall Street Journal*, June 2, 2008.

7. James Hagerty, "Amid Housing Slump, Glut Eases Slightly," *Wall Street Journal*, July 29, 2008.

8. "Operating Fundamentals Remain Steady for Independent Living and Assisted Living during the First Quarter of 2008," www.nic.org, July 15, 2008.

Chapter Eight: The Condominium Market

1. Steve Bergsman, "Is There a Condominium Bubble?," *Multifamily Trends*, September/October 2005.

2. Miller Samuel Inc. "Manhattan Market Overview: Jump in prices as Number of Sales Fall," www.millersamuel.com, March 2008.

3. Haddow & Company. "Key Condominium Market Indicators—Intown Atlanta." www.haddowandcompany.com.

4. Ibid.

5. "Comparison of Ownership vs. Rental Costs in 100 U.S. Cities Demonstrates That Rental Options Should Be a Consideration in Housing Proposals," www.cepr.net, May 8, 2008.

6. Ibid.

7. Chicago Condo Online. "Market Overview," www.chicagocondosonline.com, April 1, 2008.

8. Ibid.

9. Jules Marling, "Buying a Busted Condo Development: Opportunities and Risks," www.rerc.com, Winter 2008.

Chapter Nine: Homeowner Insurance and Property Taxes

1. Gardner Selby, "Four Years after Emergency, Texas Still No. 1 in Homeowner Insurance Costs," *Austin American-Statesman*, April 24, 2007.

2. Jim Hickey, "Vineyarders Join State House Outcry over Coastal Home Insurance Crisis," *Vineyard Gazette*, June 1, 2007.

3. Ibid.

4. Florida Tax Watch. "Controlling Escalating Property Taxation and Local Government Spending and Revenue," www.floridataxwatch.org, December 2006.

Chapter Ten: Urban and Suburban Infill

1. Sudeep Reddy, "Gasoline Hits Average of $4 a Gallon," *Wall Street Journal*, June 9, 2008.

2. Richard Haughey, Urban Land Institute. "Urban Infill Housing: Myth and Fact," www.uli.org, 2001.

3. Jose Valcourt and Justin Scheck, "How to Ease Cost of Commuting," *Wall Street Journal*, May 29, 2008.

4. Ana Campoy, "Prices Curtail U.S. Gasoline Use," *Wall Street Journal*, June 20, 2008.

5. Jahna Berry, "Transit Jam," *Arizona Republic,* June 9, 2008.
6. Ana Campoy and Alex Roth, "Riders Swamp Public Transit," *Wall Street Journal,* May 30, 2008.

Chapter Eleven: The Market for Second Homes

1. "Baby Boomers Drive Second Home Purchases," www.relohomesearch.com, February 28, 2006.
2. Keunwon Chung, "Resorts," www.realtor.org, March 2006.
3. Ibid.
4. "Second Home Sales Accounted for One-Third of Transactions in 2007, www .realtors.org, March 28, 2008.
5. Ibid.
6. Walter Molony, "Second-Home Owner Survey Shows Solid Market, Appetite for More," www.realtor.org, May 11, 2006.
7. "Second Home Sales Accounted for One-Third of Transactions in 2007," www .realtors.org, March 28, 2008.
8. Gary Engelhardt, "Study on Housing Trends among Baby Boomers," www .housingamerica.org, December 1, 2006.
9. Liam Bailey, 2008 Annual Wealth Report, www.knightfrank.co.uk.
10. "Second Home Sales Accounted for One-Third of Transactions in 2007," www .realtors.org, March 28, 2008.
11. Ibid.
12. Robin Goldwyn Blumenthal, "Mountains of Money," *Barron's,* February 4, 2008.

Chapter Twelve: The Market for Vacation Properties

1. Paula Hamilton, "Lodging Econometrics Announces the 2006–2007 Development Forecast for Timeshares, Condo Hotels and Hotels with Residences Specialty Sectors," www.lodgingeconometrics.com, December 13, 2005.
2. Michael Corkery, Sara Lin, and Ruth Simon, "Rooms with a Bubble View," *Wall Street Journal,* April 5–6, 2008.
3. Steve Bergsman, "Paradise Found: Demand for Second Homes Is Lifting Prices Nationwide. Why the Boom Will Last," *Barron's,* May 31, 2004.
4. Jamie Cheng, "Ultimate Resort Acquires Tanner and Haley Assets in $98 Million Deal," www.halogenguides.com, November 21, 2006.
5. Ibid.
6. "Hospitality Top Ten Thoughts for 2007," www.accord-realestate.com, February 15, 2007.
7. Tamara Audi, "Marriott Posts 28% Decline in Profits," *Wall Street Journal,* October 3, 2008.

About the Author

Steve Bergsman is a nationally recognized financial and real estate writer. For more than 25 years, he has contributed to a wide range of magazines, newspapers, and wire services, including the *New York Times*, the *Wall Street Journal Sunday*, *Global Finance*, *Executive Decision*, *Chief Executive*, *The Australian*, *Investment Dealer's Digest*, Reuters News Service, and Copley News Service. He has been a regular contributor to the "Ground Floor" real estate column in Barron's and has written for all of the leading real estate industry publications, including *National Real Estate Investor*, *Institutional Real Estate Letter*, *Retail Traffic*, *Multifamily Trends*, *Real Estate Portfolio*, *Shopping Center World*, *Mortgage Banking*, and *Urban Land*.

Bergsman's other books include:

- *Maverick Real Estate Investing: The Art of Buying and Selling Properties Like Trump, Zell, Simon, and the World's Greatest Land Owners*
- *Maverick Real Estate Financing: The Art of Raising Capital and Owning Properties Like Ross, Sanders, and Carey*
- *Passport to Exotic Real Estate: Buying U.S. and Foreign Property in Breathtaking, Beautiful, and Faraway Lands*